S0-AJT-488

Loops & Lattes

CALEDON HIKES

+ 37 LOOP ROUTES +

Nicola Ross

Woodrising
CONSULTING INC.

Copyright © 2015 Nicola Ross

Caledon Hikes: Loops & Lattes – 37 Loop Routes
Published by Woodrising Consulting Inc.
Belfountain, Ontario L7K 0E7

For ordering inquiries, please contact:
www.nicolaross.ca
nross@woodrising.com

Library and Archives Canada Cataloguing in Publication

Ross, Nicola, author
   Caledon hikes : loops & lattes : 37 loop routes / Nicola Ross.

ISBN 978-0-9940302-0-7 (pbk.)

1. Hiking – Ontario – Caledon – Guidebooks.
2. Trails – Ontario – Caledon – Guidebooks.
3. Caledon (Ont.) – Guidebooks. I. Title.

GV199.44.C22C21 2015   796.5109713'535   C2015-902560-5

Cover painting by Julian Mulock
Design by Gillian Stead
All photographs and maps by Nicola Ross unless otherwise noted.

Printed in Canada by Friesens on FSC certified paper.

For Alex

Contents

Bridge over the Credit River near Belfountain.
PHOTO BY ANGELA LARSON

The Loops *continued*

Foreword

Hiking trails are a many splendored thing. As the founding members of the 20-year-old Humber Valley Heritage Trail Association recognized, a trail raises public awareness. This, they've discovered, translates into demand for environmental and cultural protection. Similarly, over 50 years ago, the Bruce Trail Conservancy recognized that a trail would increase the number of people who appreciate and connect with nature. This, they've discovered, results in improved stewardship of the Niagara Escarpment. Since 1994, the visionaries behind the Caledon Trailway recognized how a trail offers recreational enjoyment. This, they've discovered, helps make Caledon a healthy, vibrant community.

The threads linking Caledon's hiking trails include commitment, respect, volunteering, zest for being active in the great outdoors and an inspiring landscape. Without these attributes, Nicola Ross's new book, *Caledon Hikes: Loops & Lattes*, could have never come to be. The fact this exciting new guide overflows with wonderful hiking opportunities along fabulous loop routes is proof that Caledon is indeed a strong and vibrant community.

As you explore the trails profiled by Nicola, consider saying a heartfelt thank you to the organizations and the hundreds of volunteers that contribute to your hiking enjoyment.

Philip Gosling
BRUCE TRAIL CONSERVANCY

Emil Kolb
CALEDON TRAILWAY

Dan O'Reilly
HUMBER VALLEY HERITAGE TRAIL ASSOCIATION

Introduction

Walking has created paths, roads, trade routes, generated local and cross-continental senses of place, shaped cities, parks, generated maps, guidebooks, gear, and, further afield, a vast library of walking stories and poems, of pilgrimages, mountaineering expeditions, meanders, and summer picnics.

REBECCA SOLNIT, *Wanderlust: A History of Walking*

In tackling *Caledon Hikes: Loops & Lattes*, I married three of my passions: Caledon, hiking and writing. In it, I've described 37 hikes that take from an hour to a full day, and that begin and end at the same location. If you think it's remarkable there are so many loop routes in Caledon, I agree. It is amazing. The reason is that Caledon has a unique set of ingredients: It starts with portions of the Bruce Trail, the Oak Ridges (Moraine) Trail, the Humber Valley Heritage Trail, the Grand Valley Trail and the Trans Canada Trail. Add two converted railway lines: the Caledon Trailway and the Elora Cataract Trailway, and throw in a good helping of quiet back roads and a healthy pinch of small towns and villages, as well as the Niagara Escarpment, the Oak Ridges Moraine, Credit River, Humber River and Etobicoke Creek. Then for good measure sprinkle Southern Ontario's Greenbelt over top.

When you add up these basics, it's evident that Caledon has what's needed to satisfy hikers of all skill levels. My job in *Caledon Hikes: Loops & Lattes* was to blend them together in just the right proportions so I could cook up hours of walking routes for your hiking enjoyment.

If your idea of a good outing is to walk along trails that take you deep into forests of towering maples, ash and basswoods, by farm fields green with corn and golden with wheat, across kames and kettles high on the Oak Ridges Moraine, close to crystal streams and waterfalls that crash over the Niagara Escarpment, as well as down quiet country roads that pass by century-old stone and brick houses, then *Caledon Hikes: Loops & Lattes* is for you. If you are attuned to stopping for a frosty pint or a hot coffee en route, then *Caledon Hikes: Loops & Lattes* is for you too. If your genetic makeup spurns walking in and out along the same trail, it would be best that you crack open a copy of Caledon's first-ever and only dedicated hiking guide. And if you abhor the bother of a car drop, then you'd better pick up your copy of *Caledon Hikes: Loops & Lattes* right now. It will keep you and your house guests entertained for hours, and not just because it offers so many hiking options but because it also gives you tidbits of useful and interesting information: Who was Glen Haffy? What is the Devil's Pulpit?

> *"My most memorable hikes can be classified as 'Shortcuts that Backfired'."*
> EDWARD ABBEY

Where is the best place to look for trilliums? When do the spring peepers peep? Where can I pick up home-baked cookies or a cream-cheese-laden bagel en route? What festivals are celebrated in which village and when? And after the hike is done, the route will take you right back to where you began. The circle is complete.

Toronto Life recently referred to Caledon as the Hamptons of the north, suggesting it "is not so much a town as an evocation of a fantasy – a mythological place that exists primarily in people's imaginations." Pay no mind to that city-slicker magazine. Caledon, all 700 square kilometres of it (larger than the entire City of Toronto), is very real indeed. Comprising a handful of villages and small towns occasionally interrupting what is mostly rural and agricultural land, high cliffs, soaring vistas and deep colourful woods, Caledon is a gem. Moreover, all this hiking is within an hour of Yonge and Bloor streets, 45 minutes from the lakeshore in Mississauga, 20 minutes from Brampton, 10 from Orangeville.

Cheltenham Badlands. PHOTO BY GARY HALL

I invite you to enjoy every one of the 37 hikes included in *Caledon Hikes: Loops & Lattes*. You might even undertake the 4-day / 3-night Grand Caledon Tour, which links Belfountain, Terra Cotta, Cheltenham, Bolton, Palgrave, Caledon East and Inglewood. I've used my knowledge of the landscape and the culture to make all the routes described in this book interesting, to provide you with clear directions and enough snippets of Caledon's past and present to bring the countryside to life. I've even suggested the best spots for the most satisfying lattes and the dreamiest ice cream cones. It's a pleasure to share Caledon's landscape, my knowledge and passion for it.

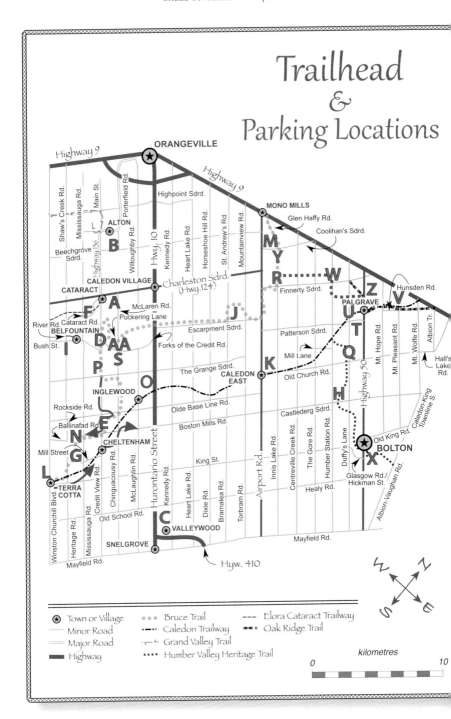

Trailhead & Parking Locations

Trailhead & Parking Locations

LOOP #	Parking	LOOP NAME	LOOP #	Parking	LOOP NAME
Loop 1	T	Albion Hills Red Loop	Loop 20	n/a	Hockley Valley/Jeju Olle Loop (see p 107)
Loop 2	B	Alton Grange/Upper Credit Loop	Loop 21	n/a	Hockley Valley Short Loop (see p 111)
Loop 3	B	Alton Pinnacle Loop	Loop 22	H	Humber River/Duffy's Lane Loop
Loop 4	I	Belfountain/Crow's Nest Loop	Loop 23	O	Inglewood/Ken Whillans Loop
Loop 5	I	Belfountain/Forks Park Loop	Loop 24	P	Judy Meredith Equestrian Loop
Loop 6	I	Belfountain/Judy Charbonneau Loop	Loop 25	P	Long Badlands/Devil's Pulpit Loop
Loop 7	D	Belfountain Luckenuf Loop	Loop 26	S	McLaren Loop
Loop 8	X	Bolton Loop	Loop 27	A	Moraine Meets Escarpment Loop
Loop 9	K	Caledon East Loop	Loop 28	V	Oak Ridges Moraine Loop
Loop 10	F	Cataract Loop	Loop 29	Z	Palgrave Combo Loop
Loop 11	E	Cheltenham Badlands Mini Loop	Loop 30	W	Palgrave Forest Humber Loop
Loop 12	G	Cheltenham Village Loop	Loop 31	U	Palgrave Village Loop
Loop 13	P	Devil's Pulpit/Paula Coats Loop	Loop 32	N	Rockside Loop
Loop 14	Q	Duffy's Lane/Albion Hills Loop	Loop 33	J	St. Andrew's Church Loop
Loop 15	AA	Forks Park/Brimstone Loop	Loop 34	L	Terra Cotta Loop
Loop 16	A	Forks Park/Meadow Loop	Loop 35	R	The Dingle/Don Mitchell Loop
Loop 17	Y	Glen Haffy Loop	Loop 36	R	The Dingle/Palgrave Long Loop
Loop 18	M	Glen Haffy Red, Green & Blue Loop	Loop 37	C	Valleywood Loop
Loop 19	n/a	Grand Caledon Tour Loop (see p 103)			

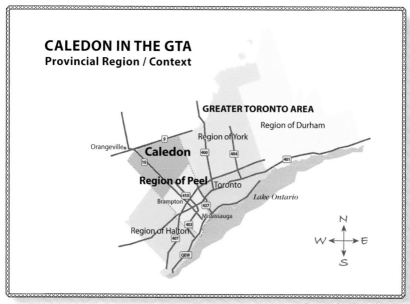

CALEDON IN THE GTA
Provincial Region / Context

GREATER TORONTO AREA

Region of Durham

Orangeville

Region of York

Caledon

Region of Peel

Toronto

Brampton

Lake Ontario

Mississauga

Region of Halton

Courtesy of the Town of Caledon

15

How to Use this Guide

Consider

Levels of Difficulty

Easy

Moderate

Challenging

✦ *What length of hike do you want?* The hikes are ordered both alphabetically and by their length, from shortest (about 1 hour) to longest (up to about 9 hours). (Plus the Grand Caledon Tour.)

✦ *How difficult a hike do you want?* The description for each hike tells you whether it is EASY (mostly flat with good footing), MODERATE (some hills and/or rocky and uneven terrain) or CHALLENGING (lots of hills and/or rocky and uneven terrain).

✦ *What type of hike would you prefer?* Do you want to walk along a forested trail on the Niagara Escarpment or meander through open hummocky terrain on the Oak Ridges Moraine? You can stay away from roads altogether or follow a route that takes you through a picturesque village.

✦ *Do you want to carry a picnic or stop along the way at a restaurant, café or general store?* The description for each hike tells you if there is somewhere to stop en route for food and/or drinks.

Refer to the Guide

✦ Look at the Loop Legend (pages 20 & 21) and find the hikes that are a suitable length and level of difficulty.

✦ Read the description to determine which of the suitable routes offers your preferred way of keeping your feet and stomach happy.

✦ Read through the Overview, Directions and Nicola's Insider Info for the routes that are the right for you.

✦ Select your route.

✦ Refer to the Trailhead & Parking Locations map (page 14). It shows you where to park and begin (and end) your selected route.

✦ Win a prize. The last item in "Nicola's Insider Info" for each hike is a small photograph under the heading "GPS Trail Marker." For instructions on how to use your GPS or camera to win prizes by identifying the location of or taking a photo of these markers, visit **nicolaross.ca**.

GPS

What You Need to Know About Hiking in Caledon

✦ All the routes in this guide follow established trails or roads that are accessible to the public. If you want to keep having access to these routes respect the land and stay on the trail.

✦ Maintaining access to public lands often requires diligent effort by citizens. Get to know what lands around you are public, and ensure they are protected for public use and/or environmental stewardship.

✦ Where these routes follow roads, they are almost always quiet back roads with minimal traffic. Occasionally, I've had to include a short walk on a busy road to close the loop.

✦ Understand how to "read" the blazes used by the Bruce Trail, Humber Valley Heritage Trail and Oak Ridges Trail. (*See Figure 1.*)

✦ Please tell me about your hiking experiences on these loops. Write to nross@woodrising.com or visit nicolaross.ca.

✦ Support the agencies and organizations that build and maintain the trails. Buy a membership to the Bruce Trail Conservancy, the Oak Ridges Trail Association, the Humber Valley Heritage Trail Association and/or the Grand Valley Trail Association.

✦ If you are a member of the Bruce Trail Conservancy, you can walk along the Bruce Trail as it passes through the Belfountain and Terra Cotta conservation areas without paying the entrance fee. If you park your car or want to use these areas for anything other than hiking the Bruce Trail, you do have to pay the entrance fee.

THE BLAZES

| Turn Right | Turn Left | Straight On | Trail Ends |

Figure 1

Cattle near Palgrave anticipating weather.

✦ For all Credit Valley Conservation conservation areas, including Belfountain, Ken Whillans and Terra Cotta, they are now offering "FREE Active Transportation Entrance." This means that if you can bike, walk, run, skateboard, etc. to one of their conservation areas you receive free admission during their posted hours of operation.

✦ In Caledon, dogs must be on a leash. Keep your dog under control. Stoop and scoop if they deposit on a trail, sidewalk or someone's lawn.

✦ Wear comfortable clothes, a hat and running or hiking shoes. The trails can be slippery so take care.

✦ Don't litter.

✦ Learn to recognize poison ivy.

✦ Park in the designated areas described in this guide.

✦ Carry bug juice, sunscreen, a bit of cash and water.

✦ When walking on a road without much of a shoulder, cross over to the right side if going up a blind hill or around the inside of a corner. It's safer.

The Loops

Loop Routes — BY DISTANCE

Loop #	Loop Route Name	Closest Town/Village	Start/End Point	Parking Location	Length (km)	Hiking Time	* Level of Difficulty	Page #
16	Forks Park/ Meadow Loop	Coulterville	Forks of Credit Parking Lot on McLaren Rd	A	2	30-45 minutes	1	91
3	Alton Pinnacle Loop	Alton	Alton Mill Arts Centre Rear Parking Lot	B	2.7	45 minutes to 1 hr	2	31
37	Valleywood Loop	Snelgrove	Newhouse Park in Valleywood	C	2.8	45 minutes to 1 hr	1	179
7	Belfountain Luckenuf Loop	Belfountain	Belfountain Conservation Area	D	3	45 minutes to 1 hr	2	51
11	Cheltenham Badlands Mini Loop	Cheltenham	Credit View Rd south of Olde Base Line Rd	E	3.3	45 minutes to 1 hr	1	69
10	Cataract Loop	Coulterville	Mississauga Rd & Cataract Rd	F	4	1 to 1½ hrs	1	65
12	Cheltenham Village Loop	Cheltenham	Brickyards Parking Lot on Mississauga Rd & Mill St	G	4.5	1 to 1½ hrs	1	73
22	Humber River/ Duffy's Lane Loop	Palgrave/ Caledon East	Castlederg Sdrd between Humber Station Rd & Duffy's Lane	H	4.7	1¼ to 1½ hrs	1	113
4	Belfountain/ Crow's Nest Loop	Belfountain	Shaw's Creek Rd & River Rd	I	5.2	1¼ to 1¾ hrs	2	35
33	St. Andrew's Church Loop	Caledon East	Escarpment Sdrd between St. Andrew's Rd & Mountainview Rd	J	5.2	1¼ to 1¾ hrs	1	163
9	Caledon East Loop	Caledon East	Caledon East Community Complex on Old Church Rd	K	5.7	1½ to 2 hrs	1	61
34	Terra Cotta Loop	Terra Cotta	Terra Cotta Conservation Area Parking Lot	L	5.7	1½ to 2 hrs	2	167
18	Glen Haffy Red, Green & Blue Loop	Mono Mills	Glen Haffy Conservation Area Lookout Point Parking Lot	M	5.8	1½ to 2 hrs	2	99
21	Hockley Valley Short Loop	Orangeville	Hockley Rd between 2nd & 3rd lines EHS of Mono	n/a	5.9	1½ to 2 hrs	2	111
32	Rockside Loop	Terra Cotta	Boston Mills Rd west of Mississauga Rd	N	5.9	1½ to 2 hrs	2	159
27	Moraine Meets Escarpment Loop	Coulterville	Forks of Credit Park Lot on McLaren Rd	A	6.8	1½ to 2½ hrs	2	135
23	Inglewood/Ken Whillans Loop	Inglewood	Inglewood in Lot by Caledon Trailway	O	7.2	1½ to 2½ hrs	1	117
14	Duffy's Lane/ Albion Hills Loop	Palgrave/ Caledon East	Duffy's Lane north of Old Church Rd	Q	8	2 to 3 hrs	1	81

* LEVELS OF DIFFICULTY: 1 Easy • 2 Moderate • 3 Challenging
n/a: Parking for the two Hockley loops is on Hockley Road north of Orangeville between Highway 10 and Airport Road.

Loop Routes — BY DISTANCE

Loop #	Loop Route Name	Closest Town/Village	Start/End Point	Parking Location	Length (km)	Hiking Time	* Level of Difficulty	Page #
13	Devil's Pulpit/ Paula Coats Loop	Inglewood	Credit View Rd north of The Grange Sdrd	P	8	2 to 3 hrs	3	77
35	The Dingle/ Don Mitchell Loop	Palgrave	Innis Lake Rd north of Finnerty Sdrd	R	8	2 to 3 hrs	1	171
26	McLaren Loop	Inglewood	McLaren Rd south of Forks of Credit Rd	S	8.4	2 to 3 hrs	2	131
6	Belfountain/Judy Charbonneau Loop	Belfountain	Shaw's Creek Rd & River Rd	I	8.5	2 to 3 hrs	2	45
1	Albion Hills Red Loop	Palgrave	Cedar Grove 1 Parking Lot in Albion Hills Conservation Area	T	9	2 to 3 hrs	1	23
31	Palgrave Village Loop	Palgrave	Palgrave Forest & Wildlife Area Parking Lot on Duffys Lane north of Patterson Sdrd	U	9.3	2½ to 3½ hrs	1	153
28	Oak Ridges Moraine Loop	Palgrave	Caledon Trailway on Mount Pleasant Rd south of Hwy 9	V	9.5	2½ to 3½ hrs	2	139
30	Palgrave Forest Humber Loop	Palgrave	Humber Station Rd & Finnerty Sdrd	W	9.6	2½ to 3½ hrs	1	149
8	Bolton Loop	Bolton	Edelweiss Park on Glasgow Rd	X	9.7	2½ to 3½ hrs	2	55
2	Alton Grange/ Upper Credit Loop	Alton	Parking Lot on Cardwell St in Alton	B	9.8	2½ to 3½ hrs	1	27
24	Judy Meredith Equestrian Loop	Inglewood	Credit View Rd north of The Grange Sdrd	P	10.5	2½ to 3½ hrs	2	121
17	Glen Haffy Loop	Mono Mills	Coolihans Sdrd & Glen Haffy Rd	Y	10.7	2½ to 3½ hrs	2	95
29	Palgrave Combo Loop	Palgrave	Palgrave Rotary Park on east side of Hwy 50 north of Palgrave	Z	10.9	2½ to 3½ hrs	2	145
20	Hockley Valley/ Jeju Olle Loop	Orangeville	Hockley Rd between 2nd & 3rd lines EHS of Mono	n/a	11.6	3 to 4 hrs	3	107
15	Forks Park/ Brimstone Loop	Brimstone/ Inglewood	McLaren Rd north of Forks of Credit Rd	AA	12.8	3 to 4½ hrs	2	85
5	Belfountain/ Forks Park Loop	Belfountain	Shaw's Creek Rd & River Rd	I	13.3	3½ to 4½ hrs	2	39
25	Long Badlands/ Devil's Pulpit Loop	Inglewood/ Cheltenham	Credit View Rd north of The Grange Sdrd	P	18.2	4½ to 6+ hrs	3	125
36	The Dingle/Palgrave Long Loop	Palgrave	Innis Lake Rd north of Finnerty Sdrd	R	25	6 to 9 hrs	2	175
19	Grand Caledon Loop	Various	Be sure to park in a designated parking area	n/a	121	4 days	3	103

* LEVELS OF DIFFICULTY: **1** Easy • **2** Moderate • **3** Challenging

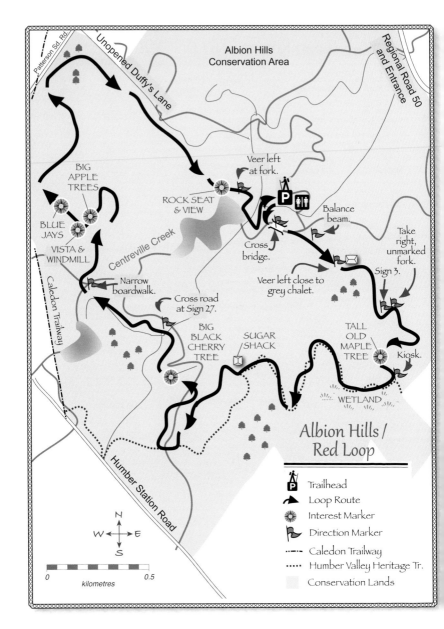

Albion Hills
Conservation Area

Unopened Duffy's Lane

Patterson Sd. Rd.

Regional Road 50
and Entrance

Veer left
at fork.

ROCK SEAT
& VIEW

BIG
APPLE
TREES

Balance
beam.

Take
right,
unmarked
fork.
Sign 3.

BLUE
JAYS

Cross
bridge.

VISTA &
WINDMILL

Centreville Creek

Veer left close to
grey chalet.

Caledon Trailway

Narrow
boardwalk.

Cross road
at Sign 27.

BIG
BLACK
CHERRY
TREE

SUGAR
SHACK

TALL
OLD
MAPLE
TREE

Kiosk.

WETLAND

Humber Station Road

Albion Hills /
Red Loop

🚶P Trailhead
🏃 Loop Route
✳ Interest Marker
🚩 Direction Marker
–·–·– Caledon Trailway
······ Humber Valley Heritage Tr.
▨ Conservation Lands

N
W   E
S

0   0.5
kilometres

*"Returning home is the most difficult part of long-distance hiking.
You have grown outside the puzzle and your piece no longer fits."*

CINDY ROSS

22

Albion Hills Red Loop

Avoid this hike on Tuesday evenings and during the summer solstice (around June 21) due to mountain bike events.

OVERVIEW

This loop is entirely along a mostly level, dry and sandy footpath. No roads to contend with. The Red Trail meanders through lovely woods, by ponds and near wetlands. The farther you travel, the deeper you will be in nature, solitude and peace. The route takes you past big old black cherry trees, mature apples and some mammoth maples. Keep your eyes peeled for these old-growth trees that have eluded the razor-sharp edge of a double-bitted axe.

It might be a bit raucous when you start off, but have faith. Within minutes you leave behind the sound of banshees disguised as kids cannonballing into the swimming pool. The ensuing silence is that much more precious given how things began.

Follow the red arrows for the Red Trail from beginning to end. Sounds easy, but the red markers desert you in a few spots, and it may take some sleuthing to find the next red arrow. When you find it keep going. But if the next arrow is another colour, retrace your footsteps and try a different path.

1

Nicola's Insider Info

LENGTH
9 kilometres

LEVEL OF DIFFICULTY
Easy

LENGTH OF TIME
2 to 3 hours

NUMBER OF STEPS
11,984

kCAL BURNED 386

HIGHLIGHTS
Peace seems to increase as you walk

PLACES TO EAT/DRINK
Palgrave Café (closed Sundays), Palgrave Variety Store, The Church pub (Wed to Sun, 4pm to 12pm)

ENTRANCE FEE
Adult $6.50/Seniors $5.50/<14 free

GPS

TRAIL MARKER
Loop 1

TERRY CARR MEMORIAL TRAIL
WHITE BREASTED NUTHATCH
Sitta carolinensis

Albion Hills

Directions

1. Enter the main entrance of the Albion Hills Conservation Area on the west side of Highway 50 just south of Palgrave. The entrance fee is Adult $6.50/Seniors $5.50/<14 free. Pick up a trail map on your way in.

2. Park in the Cedar Grove 1 lot where there is an information kiosk.

3. Walk toward Cedar Grove 2. There are washrooms on your left and an old stone water fountain beside a drinking water tap.

4. The Red Trail is just ahead. Follow it to the left since all arrows and information along the route are set up for this clockwise direction.

5. The trail parallels a quiet stream on your right and comes to a bridge. Not long afterwards, you come to a balance beam over a muddy spot. Intended for mountain cyclists, I had to try it on foot. A lot of mountain biking goes on and you pass by plenty of dedicated bicycle routes. While this trail is wide in most places, keep an eye open for mountain bikes.

6. The trail arrives at a spot where there is a grey building on your left called the Albion Hills Chalet. It is used for weddings and other events. The trail disappears here. The most obvious route goes straight ahead crossing another trail before passing under some big maples. *This is NOT your route.* Veer left and walk closer to the chalet. When you are just past the chalet look for a red arrow up ahead across an open field. In late summer, the grass can obscure this arrow so it may take a few tries to find it.

7. When you pick it up, you enter the forest. The trail is well marked along this stretch, though just after Sign 3, you need to take the right fork that wasn't marked (in 2014).

8. Keep your eyes open for some big old-growth maples. They have huge girths and gnarly old bark.

9. A little more than 1k from the chalet, you come to a kiosk. The Humber Valley Heritage Trail/Oak Ridges Trail joins the Red Trail here. For a while you follow both red arrows and white blazes.

10. You pass by a lovely wetland favoured by waterfowl. After about 1.5k (from the kiosk), you come to a maple-sugar shack. Sap from maple trees is boiled down, reducing its volume by about 20 times, to make the best part of a pancake breakfast.

11. By now, you likely have settled into this trail. The footing is great and you are far from the madding crowd. Keep following the red arrows. Over the next 2k, you pass a huge black cherry tree with dark shaggy bark, cross a small road and walk along a narrow set of boardwalks. Take a moment to read the interpretive signs.

12. After you leave the forest, you find a lovely vista that looks over an open valley. To your left is a lone windmill. Look for some mature apple trees, a sure sign that cattle once grazed here. I came across a large flock of blue jays (*Cyanocitta cristata*). These easily recognizable birds are omnivorous. In addition to eating seeds, they consume mice, frogs and even other birds. Put that on your birdfeeder next winter.

Black cherry trees have dark bark that is scaly.

13. You have another kilometre of uninterrupted trail until you come to an unopened section of Duffy's Lane, which you parallel for a while.

14. A few hundred metres after leaving Duffy's Lane, you come to a rock bench that looks over a large pond. Farther away is the screeching pool, as I like to call it. Take a moment to brace yourself for your return to civilization. At the next fork in the trail, veer left.

15. Stay with the red arrows, crossing a road passing from Sign 42 to Sign 20. After Sign 20 you come to the stone fountain and water tap. Turn left here and return to your car.

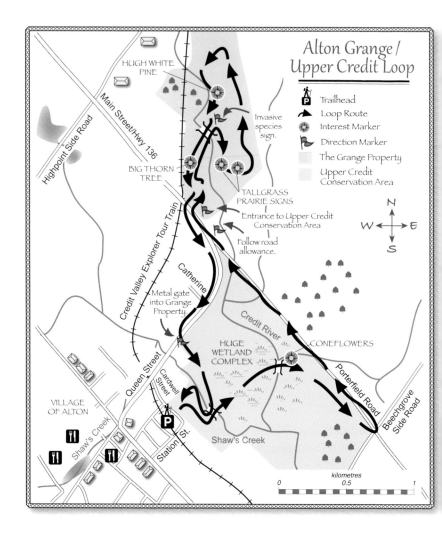

Alton Grange / Upper Credit Loop

P Trailhead
Loop Route
Interest Marker
Direction Marker
The Grange Property
Upper Credit Conservation Area

HUGH WHITE PINE

Main Street/Hwy 136

Highpoint Side Road

Invasive species sign.

BIG THORN TREE

TALLGRASS PRAIRIE SIGNS

Entrance to Upper Credit Conservation Area

Follow road allowance.

Credit Valley Explorer Tour Train

Catherine

Metal gate into Grange Property

Credit River

HUGE WETLAND COMPLEX

CONEFLOWERS

Porterfield Road

Beechgrove Side Road

Queen Street

Cardwell Street

VILLAGE OF ALTON

Shaw's Creek

P

Station St.

Shaw's Creek

N
W E
S

kilometres
0   0.5   1

"No city should be too large
for a man to walk out in the morning."
CYRIL CONNOLLY

Alton Grange / Upper Credit Loop

Best done in the autumn when those pesky mosquitos have disappeared.

OVERVIEW

This is a great fall hike. The extensive wetlands in The Grange Property that you cross following a set of long boardwalks will be bug-free, and the trail through the Upper Credit Conservation Area, which primarily crosses gorgeous open fields, will be sunny and bright. Wait for a day with clear blue skies and then enjoy that last bit of warmth on your back and shoulders.

Owned by the Ministry of Natural Resources and managed by the Alton Grange Association, a non-profit volunteer organization, The Grange Property comprises 142 hectares that are adjacent to the village of Alton. The property contains spectacular wetlands and both Shaw's Creek and the Credit River. You get to walk right through areas that are magnets for birds, amphibians and reptiles.

A bit of busy highway links the two parts of this loop. Just grin and bear it. If you can't put up with the highway, park in the lot for the Upper Credit Conservation Area just northeast of Alton, and only walk that portion of the trail. It will take you about an hour and avoids the road walking.

Nicola's Insider Info

LENGTH
9.8 kilometres

LEVEL OF DIFFICULTY
Easy

LENGTH OF TIME
2.5 to 3.5 hours

NUMBER OF STEPS
12,757

kCAL BURNED 425

HIGHLIGHTS
Wetland complex, open fields with a wide, well-maintained trail

PLACES TO EAT/DRINK
None en route.
Alton has Bryant's General Store, Ray's 3rd Generation Bistro Bakery, the Millcroft Inn and Shaw's Creek Café in the Alton Mill Arts Centre.

ENTRANCE FEE
n/a

GPS

TRAIL MARKER
Loop 2

Directions

1. On Cardwell Street, a small back street on the far east end of Alton, there is a parking lot. You enter it through a gate where there is a sign announcing this is The Grange Property. Park here.

2. The trail exits the parking lot at the end opposite the entrance.

3. Follow the trail as it makes a sharp right turn and passes a sign with symbols that tell you what activities are allowed on the trail. When you come to a Y-intersection just after the activity sign, veer left. You pass through the first of many wetlands.

4. After 400m, you cross over a metal bridge that spans Shaw's Creek and enter a cedar forest. Shaw's Creek was the main millstream in Alton, providing power for a series of woolen mills, two of which have been renovated – one into the lovely Millcroft Inn and the other into the busy Alton Mill Arts Centre. Shaw's Creek flows into the Credit River.

5. Upon entering the cedar forest, the trail splits, going straight ahead and to the right. Turn right and begin following the blue blazes that mark this section of the trail.

6. Again you pass through beautiful wetlands. You come to another small bridge, which crosses over the Credit River as it makes its way from north of Orangeville to meet the West Credit River at the Forks of the Credit. On the far side of the bridge look for elegant tall yellow coneflowers in the summer.

7. Keep following the blue blazes until the trail comes to a quiet gravel road. Turn left here on to Porterfield Road and go north. It's a peaceful walk along this stretch.

8. When you see the busy paved road (Main Street/Hwy 136), keep walking straight ahead up the old road allowance until it meets the highway. You only have to walk for 200m with cars whizzing by.

9. After 200m along the highway, turn right into the Upper Credit Conservation Area. Take a look at the map at the information kiosk and pick up one of the booklets if available.

10. Follow the Entrance Trail past the metal gate. The trail is well maintained and wide. Note: this is a popular place to walk dogs and not all owners use leashes. It can be well "dogulated" along the first part of the trail.

11. Look over open fields and some lovely homes to the north before the trail drops into a shallow valley and you cross a bridge over the Credit River.

Big old thorn tree along the route.

12. Just after the bridge, you come to a T-intersection of trails where there is an information sign about invasive species. Turn right here. The trails in this conservation area are not blazed, but this is the green trail as depicted on the kiosk map.

13. The trail passes an area where an information sign indicates the conservation authority is rehabilitating some tallgrass prairie, which is very exciting.

14. Stay with the trail until you come to another sign about tallgrass prairie. Turn right here and then left. You will now be following a fence line. You pass between two elegant elm trees, survivors of the Dutch Elm Disease. Tallgrass Ontario says rehabilitating Southern Ontario's tallgrass prairie is challenging because less than 2% of the land is publicly owned and this region is home to more species at risk than any other in the country.

15. The trail is easy to follow as it turns left and then left again. It then drops down into a forest by the river. As you leave the forest, look for the mammoth white pine to your right.

16. About 300m past the white pine, you come back to the original T-intersection of trails. Turn right at the information sign about invasive species and cross the bridge back over the Credit River.

17. Follow the Entrance Trail back to the parking area and kiosk. Along the way, look for a big old thorn tree.

18. Keep walking out the entrance to the highway (Main Street/Hwy 136) and turn left toward Alton.

19. Follow the highway around a large bend to the right, passing by Porterfield Road.

20. Look for a metal gate on your left where there is a sign that says Grange Property. It is 1k from the Upper Credit Parking lot to this gate.

21. Turn left passing through an opening beside the gate. Follow the blue blazes. You may also see a few green blazes.

22. About 600m after re-entering The Grange Property, the blue blazes tell you to make a sharp left-hand turn. DO NOT TURN HERE. Follow the trail that goes straight ahead and over the bridge. If the bridge looks familiar, it's because you crossed it in the other direction. There are no blazes on this section of trail.

23. At the "Y" in the trail, veer right and then follow the path straight past the activity sign until you return to the parking lot.

Alton Pinnacle Loop

OVERVIEW

This is my favourite village loop. It combines a sweeping view of Alton and its environs from the lofty Pinnacle, with a wander past the stylish and historic Millcroft Inn, a visit to the Alton Mill Arts Centre and a walk past beautiful old homes on – move over Toronto – Caledon's own Queen Street W. Housed in an ancient woolen mill, the Alton Mill Arts Centre buzzes with the creative energy of local painters, photographers, sculptors and more. See what they have on display or watch the choreographed moves of a working potter or a painter who is adding a dash of light to complete a landscape painting.

Hungry? Stop for a snack, coffee, lunch or dinner in a variety of places including Ray's 3rd Generation Bistro Bakery, the Millcroft Inn or Shaw's Creek Café, which is located within the Alton Mill Arts Centre. You can spend a night or two at the luxurious Millcroft Inn. Housed in an old woolen mill, it is one of Ontario's finest hotels.

On this economical 45-minute loop, you walk, climb, snoop, eat, drink and shop – all while breathing fresh country air.

"Details of the many walks I made along the crest have blurred, now, into a pleasing tapestry of grass and space and sunlight."

COLIN FLETCHER

Nicola's Insider Info

LENGTH
2.7 kilometres

LEVEL OF DIFFICULTY
Moderate

LENGTH OF TIME
45 minutes to 1 hour

NUMBER OF STEPS
3,482

kCAL BURNED 135

HIGHLIGHTS
The Pinnacle, Millcroft Inn, Alton Mill Arts Centre, homes on Queen St. W.

PLACES TO EAT/DRINK
Bryant's General Store, Ray's 3rd Generation Bistro Bakery, the Millcroft Inn and Shaw's Creek Café in the Alton Mill Arts Centre *(Alton Mill Arts Centre is open Wed to Sun and holiday Mondays from 10am to 5pm.)*

ENTRANCE FEE
n/a

TRAIL MARKER
Loop 3

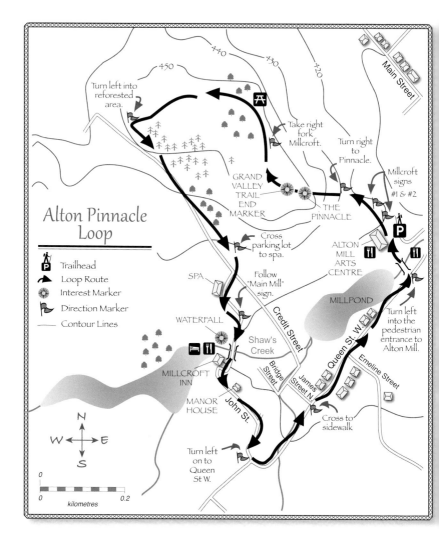

Directions

1. Park in the parking area at the Alton Mill Arts Centre (1402 Queen Street in Alton). Please use the lot farthest from the Alton Mill.

2. Begin your hike by walking from the parking area toward the Alton Mill. Look for a bronze sculpture of a scarecrow. It says you are on the Bruce Trail, but this is incorrect. Look here for a white sign that points up the hill and says "Millcroft Inn." Follow it away from the Alton Mill and up into the forest.

3. Pass by a second sign for the Millcroft Inn. When you come to a trail that is not signposted, veer right. Just ahead there is another sign that points left to the Millcroft and straight to The Pinnacle. Go straight to The Pinnacle, following the well-worn path that goes up a steep but short incline. According to *Wikimapia*, a "pinnacle" is a "mountain." Many a Banff resident might take exception to this designation for Alton's pinnacle, but this spot is very close to the highest point in Caledon. At 485m, it is just 20m short of the highest spot, which is a bit further north. (Banff sits at almost 1500m.)

4. There is a great sitting rock on The Pinnacle that allows you to look over the landscape while catching your breath. Once you do, continue up a little farther.

5. On your right look for a small white triangular sign that says "Grand Valley Trail" in pale blue letters. Below it are two white blazes that form a 'T.' This is the end, and beginning, of the Grand Valley Trail. It runs for 275k through the Grand River watershed joining Alton to Port Maitland on Lake Erie. The Grand River is one of four rivers with their headwaters in Headwaters Country. The others are the Credit, the Nottawasaga and the Humber.

6. Continue past this marker until you come to a fork in the path. Take the right fork that says it's the "long way" to the Millcroft Inn.

7. There is a picnic table here for you to enjoy. You are now walking on land owned by the Millcroft Inn, and the management has given you permission to cross their land. The inn maintains these trails. Please pay special respect to the Millcroft Inn by ensuring your dog is on a leash.

8. Just before a gravel road, the trail turns a sharp left and enters a reforested area. If you come to the road, you've gone too far.

9. Less than 500m later, the trail comes to a small road and a parking lot. Cross the parking lot heading toward some buildings. These are all part of the Millcroft Inn, and the largest is a spa.

10. At the spa, turn left and follow the road. You will see a sign directing you to the "Main Mill." Follow it as it heads down a gentle slope toward a small bridge. From the bridge look to your right. A waterfall thunders down beside the Millcroft Inn's dining room. This is Shaw's Creek, a tributary to the Credit River. It was once one of Caledon's most powerful millstreams.

The Millcroft Inn.

11. Continue on the paved road (this is John Street), passing between the conference centre and the Millcroft Inn's main entrance. One of Ontario's most spectacular inns, the Millcroft is housed in an old woolen factory. Built in 1881, it was converted into a hotel in the 1970s. The Millcroft Inn is a member of the Vintage Hotels group.

12. Once past the main building, look for the Manor House on your left. Pass it and follow John Street until it ends at Queen Street W.

13. Turn left on to Queen Street W. When you come to James Street, cross the road because there is a sidewalk on the south side of Queen Street W.

14. Follow Queen Street W past some lovely old homes. On your left is a large millpond where an annual old-timers' hockey tournament that pits village against village takes place on Family Day each winter.

15. After about 500m, just after the millpond ends, you arrive at a pedestrian entrance for the Alton Mill Arts Centre. Turn left here, crossing the bridge over Shaw's Creek. Up ahead is your vehicle.

Belfountain / Crow's Nest Loop

OVERVIEW

Village meets country on this picturesque hike since you can stop for a latte, sandwich or cold drink en route in the hamlet of Belfountain. The loop follows the Crow's Nest Side Trail in the publicly owned Willoughby Property, once the site of the Crow's Nest Quarry. You pass through a dense cedar forest that gives way to a high ridge where you look over towering maples and beech trees. Keep an eye out for jack-in-the-pulpit below the ridge. You walk alongside the West Credit River as it cascades down the Niagara Escarpment as you climb into the Belfountain Conservation Area. Once the whimsical home of C.W. Mack, it features a mini "Niagara Falls" and "Yellowstone Cave." Toss a coin in the gravity-fed, bell-topped water fountain before exiting the Belfountain Conservation Area and entering the village proper. Now it's time for a drink and sweet or savoury treats, or a look inside Belfountain's filled-to-the-rafters gift shop. If the weather allows, take your drink outside and watch this busy village percolate along.

The route is hilly and in places the footing is rough, so use good shoes and carry a hiking pole if you need one.

Nicola's Insider Info

LENGTH
5.2 kilometres

LEVEL OF DIFFICULTY
Moderate

LENGTH OF TIME
1.25 to 1.75 hours

NUMBER OF STEPS
7,201

kCAL BURNED 238

HIGHLIGHTS
Crow's Nest Quarry/ Willoughby Property, Belfountain Conservation Area, food and drink in Belfountain, Belfountain's Salamander Festival takes place the first Saturday in October.

PLACES TO EAT/DRINK
Higher Ground Coffee Co., Belfountain Inn, Caledon Hills Ice Cream Parlour

ENTRANCE FEE
Adults $5/Seniors & Children $3. No entrance fee to hikers.

TRAIL MARKER
Loop 4

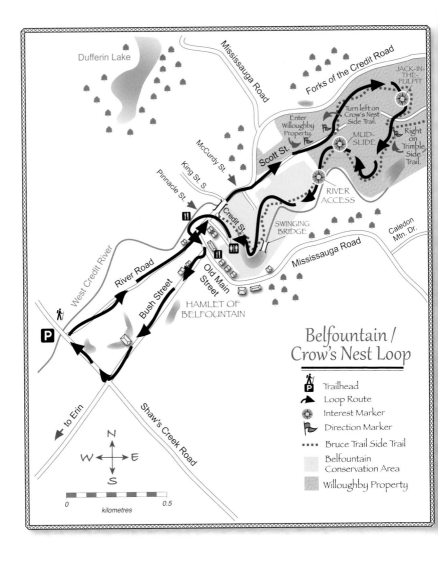

Dufferin Lake

Mississauga Road

Forks of the Credit Road

JACK-IN-THE-PULPIT

Turn left on Crow's Nest Side Trail.

Enter Willoughby Property.

MUD-SLIDE

Right on Trimble Side Trail.

McCurdy St.

Scott St.

King St. S.

Pinnacle St.

RIVER ACCESS

Credit St.

SWINGING BRIDGE

Caledon Mtn. Dr.

West Credit River

River Road

Bush Street

Old Main Street

Mississauga Road

HAMLET OF BELFOUNTAIN

P

to Erin

Shaw's Creek Road

N
W E
S

Belfountain / Crow's Nest Loop

🚶 Trailhead
➤ Loop Route
✴ Interest Marker
🚩 Direction Marker
••••• Bruce Trail Side Trail
▨ Belfountain Conservation Area
▨ Willoughby Property

0   0.5
kilometres

*"There is nothing like walking to get the feel of a country.
A fine landscape is like a piece of music; it must be taken
at the right tempo. Even a bicycle goes too fast."*

PAUL SCOTT MOWRER

Directions

(*As* Caledon Hikes *went to press there was ongoing discussion about rerouting hikers to keep them off the gravel portion of Scott Street. Look for rerouting signs or check* **www.nicolaross.ca** *for a route change.*)

1. Park on River Road where it meets Shaw's Creek Road just west of Belfountain.

2. Walk east along River Road toward Belfountain.

3. When you come to the stop sign where River Road meets Old Main Street in the village, continue walking straight ahead and go down the hill past the Belfountain Inn and the Belfountain Conservation Area.

4. Cross the bridge over the West Credit River and up out of the valley. At the top of the hill veer right (straight) on to Scott Street.

5. Follow Scott Street to the gate at #100. Enter the Willoughby Property, which is a lovely piece of public land managed by Credit Valley Conservation and owned by Ontario Heritage Trust. Bert Willoughby built the large house at the end of this road. (It is situated above the hairpin turn on the Forks of the Credit Road.) He was the Willoughby of Gibson Willoughby Ltd. Real Estate, now Royal Le Page. Pedestrians are welcome.

6. About 200m past the gate, the Crow's Nest Side Trail crosses the road. Turn left on to the trail, following its blue blazes.

7. Named for the Crow's Nest Quarry that operated here in the late 1800s, the trail enters a dark cedar forest, then climbs gently up to a narrow ridge that runs through a hardwood forest. Where you see an information sign, look for some lovely lacy hemlocks to your left.

8. About 500m from the road, the trail turns sharp right and heads down a steep but short slope. Stop at this high point and look out over the airy open forest. It's a great spot for a break and you might see white-tailed deer below.

9. Head down the trail and through a rock garden where there are lots of jack-in-the-pulpit in the spring. When I was a kid, my dad gave us 10¢ if we found a jack-in-the-pulpit. I never earned that dime, but these odd-looking flowers make me recall those days.

10. The trail passes through a grove of beech trees. Even in winter many beech saplings keep their leaves. Trees release an enzyme in fall that unglues their leaves. When trees retain them, it's called marcescence. Sometimes it's due to a killer frost, but some trees such as American beech and many oaks are prone to it. Sugar maples lose their leaves more easily.

11. The trail crosses the right-of-way (driveway), comes to a boardwalk and arrives at a trail junction. Turn left here and go down a few steps until you come to the junction with the Trimble Side Trail.

12. Turn right on the Trimble Side Trail, which is also marked by blue blazes. Roy and John Trimble, long-time Belfountain residents, ran the gas station that now houses the coffee and gift shops. Their father once ran the business as a blacksmith shop. Roy was a great naturalist who knew the area inside and out. I had the pleasure of knowing him.

13. Follow the Trimble Side Trail for 1k until you arrive at a sign indicating you are entering the Belfountain Conservation Area. You can purchase a pass (Adults $5/Children & Seniors $3) in the conservation area.

14. Look near here for a path down to a wooden bridge over the Credit River. You will not take this path, but there is a great view of the Credit River from the bridge.

15. Stay on the Trimble Side Trail (DO NOT CROSS THE BRIDGE) and climb the steps into the maintained portion of the Belfountain Conservation Area. This lovely 8-hectare site once belonged to Charles Mack, inventor of the cushion-back rubber stamp. Mack and his wife Addie purchased the property in 1908 and created a miniature "Niagara Falls" and "Yellowstone Cave," complete with stalactites hanging from the ceiling. When I was a kid, we'd dare each other to enter this damp cave. Calling his home Luckenuf, Mack also built a suspension bridge downstream from the dam and a fountain topped with a bell. Look for the stone pillars bearing the word "Luckenuf."

16. Keep following the path as it skirts the Credit River until you come to Credit Street.

17. Leave the park through the main entrance and turn left onto the Forks of the Credit Road. Head up the hill into the village. You might be tempted by the Caledon Hills Ice Cream Parlour.

18. At the village stop sign, turn right on to Bush Street and pass by the landmark brick general store. Built in 1888, it was owned for a time by former MP Garth Turner who sold it to someone who turned it into a raw food store. In 2015, it was mostly closed. The community and tourists miss the life a general store provides and hope it will soon operate again.

19. Stay on Bush Street until you arrive at Shaw's Creek Road. If it's open, drop by Moorecroft's Antiques en route.

20. Turn right on Shaw's Creek Road and follow it to River Road and your car.

Belfountain / Forks Park Loop

OVERVIEW

Any route that combines a great lunch or latte with a walk through the dramatic Forks of the Credit Park is on my list of best hikes. You start and finish near Belfountain so coffee, ice cream or other treats beckon as you hike this energetic route. It takes you down into the Forks of the Credit, along the Trimble Side Trail named after Roy and Eleanor Trimble, long-time Belfountain residents. Roy and his brother John ran the gas station for years. The same building now houses Belfountain's coffee and gift shops.

Keep a look out for a train as you pass under the trestle bridge. Then follow Dominion Street as it crosses over the spot where the Forks of the Credit gets its name, and meanders into Brimstone, a precious hamlet that was once home to some reputedly rough quarrymen. Your heart rate will rise as you climb up the Niagara Escarpment and then skirt some deep ravines before taking in the hummocky terrain of the Oak Ridges Moraine, since two of Southern Ontario's major landforms cozy up in this park. Then it's back down to the Credit River through what is arguably Caledon's most beautiful valley.

5

Nicola's
Insider Info

LENGTH
13.3 kilometres

LEVEL OF DIFFICULTY
Moderate

LENGTH OF TIME
3.5 to 4.5 hours

NUMBER OF STEPS
18,103

kCAL BURNED 595

HIGHLIGHTS
Forks of the Credit, best valley in Caledon, Brimstone, coffee, Credit River, trilliums in spring, Belfountain's Salamander Festival takes place the last Saturday in September.

PLACES TO EAT/DRINK
Higher Ground Coffee Co., Belfountain Inn, Caledon Hills Ice Cream Parlour

ENTRANCE FEE
n/a

GPS

TRAIL MARKER
Loop 5

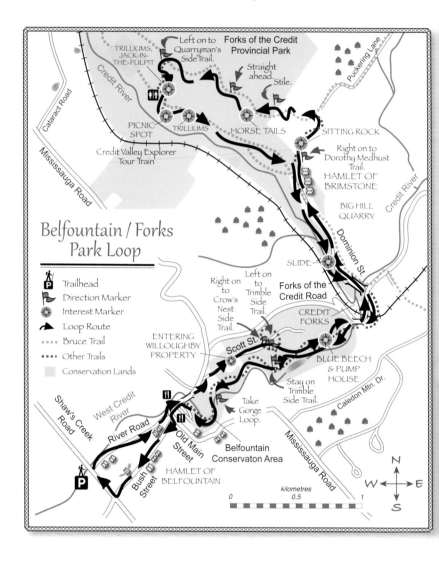

Belfountain / Forks Park Loop

Map labels:

Forks of the Credit Provincial Park

Left on to Quarryman's Side Trail.

TRILLIUMS, JACK-IN-THE-PULPIT

Straight ahead. Stile.

Puckering Lane

Credit River

Cataract Road

Mississauga Road

PICNIC SPOT

TRILLIUMS

HORSE TAILS

SITTING ROCK

Credit Valley Explorer Tour Train

Right on to Dorothy Medhust Trail.

HAMLET OF BRIMSTONE

BIG HILL QUARRY

Credit River

SLIDE

Dominion St.

Forks of the Credit Road

Right on to Crow's Nest Side Trail.

Left on to Trimble Side Trail.

CREDIT FORKS

ENTERING WILLOUGHBY PROPERTY

Scott St.

BLUE BEECH & PUMP HOUSE

Stay on Trimble Side Trail.

Caledon Mtn. Dr.

West Credit River

River Road

Shaw's Creek Road

Bush Street

Old Main Street

Take Gorge Loop.

HAMLET OF BELFOUNTAIN

Belfountain Conservaton Area

Mississauga Road

Legend:

- Trailhead
- Direction Marker
- Interest Marker
- Loop Route
- •••• Bruce Trail
- •••• Other Trails
- Conservation Lands

kilometres
0   0.5   1

N W E S

"I haven't got any special religion this morning.
My God is the God of Walkers. If you walk hard enough,
you probably don't need any other god."

BRUCE CHATWIN

Directions

(As Caledon Hikes *went to press there was ongoing discussion about rerouting hikers to keep them off the gravel portion of Scott Street. Look for rerouting signs or check* **www.nicolaross.ca** *for a route change.)*

1. Park on River Road where it meets Shaw's Creek Road just west of Belfountain.

2. Walk east along River Road toward Belfountain.

3. When you come to the stop sign where River Road meets Old Main Street in the village, walk straight ahead down the hill past the Belfountain Inn and the Belfountain Conservation Area.

4. Cross over the West Credit River and up out of the valley. At the top of the hill veer right (straight) on to Scott Street.

5. Follow Scott Street to the gate at #100. You are entering the Willoughby Property, which is a lovely piece of public land managed by Credit Valley Conservation. Pedestrians are welcome. This land was quarried in the late 1880s, well before Bert Willoughby, of Gibson Willoughby Real Estate, built an enormous house at the end of the road near the Forks of the Credit.

6. About 200m after the gate, the Crow's Nest Side Trail crosses the road. Veer right on to the Crow's Nest Side Trail, leaving the road and following the blue blazes.

7. Follow this trail for another 200m until you come to a confluence of the Crow's Nest Side Trail and the Trimble Side Trail. As you walk on a long boardwalk look for the trail junction.

8. Turn right leaving the Crow's Nest Side Trail and then almost immediately, turn left on to the Trimble Side Trail. Roy and John Trimble came to Belfountain because their father bought what is now the coffee shop and gift store. At the time, it was a blacksmith's shop that the Trimble brothers turned into a gas station and mechanic shop when cars put horses out of business. I pumped gas there as a teenager.

9. Follow the blue blazes of the Trimble Side Trail as it makes its way through a cedar forest. You skirt the top of a cliff to your right. Along the way, there is a great lookout where you can gaze over the Credit River valley. This is especially beautiful in the spring as new leaves are forming and in the fall when the trees are alive with colour.

10. As you head steadily downhill, you pass by large mounds that are actually slag piles of rubble left over from quarrying days.

11. You pass by a wooden pump house below on your right. Just past it, look back behind the pump house. See if you can make out the remains of a stone bridge. It once had train tracks over it. Trains were used to transport the enormous rocks from the quarries to the railway station that was situated at the "S" turn on the Forks of the Credit Road. My mum, now in her 90s, used to flag down the train at this station and take it into Toronto.

12. A few metres further along the trail look for a grove of blue-beech trees (*Carpinus caroliniana*). They are also known as musclewood trees because the smooth ridges on their trunks make them look like muscles, and because blue-beech is very hard. It was used to make axe handles. The most noticeable one has been partly chopped down and overhangs the trail.

13. Look out for a sharp right-hand turn that goes down some stairs before the trail empties on to the Forks of the Credit Road at a bridge that passes over the gushing West Credit River.

14. Follow the Forks of the Credit Road for 300m, passing under the trestle bridge until you come to Dominion Street. Turn left here, picking up the white blazes of the main Bruce Trail. The road is narrow as it goes under the trestle. Best to walk on the right side of the road where there is a shoulder.

15. Follow Dominion Street over a small bridge. Upstream, the west and main branches of the Credit River join, giving the area its name.

16. Before entering the hamlet of Brimstone, you pass by a spot where several large concrete blocks line the right side of the road. On September 29, 2005 after a hard downpour, the side of the hill at this point gave way. Muddy clay covered the road cutting off residents of Brimstone. Brimstone is quiet now, but it was once home to reputedly rowdy quarrymen, hence its name.

17. Just past Brimstone, you pass by a gate into the Forks of the Credit Park.

18. Almost immediately, the Dorothy Medhurst Side Trail leaves the main Bruce Trail. Take this side trail with its blue blazes as it goes to the right into the forest and begins to climb. Dorothy Medhurst was a Bruce Trail pioneer and tireless volunteer. She died in 2010, aged 95.

19. Your temples will pound as you climb up the escarpment for about 400m. Take a break when you pass by a lovely shaded "sitting rock."

20. At a well-marked spot, the Dorothy Medhurst Side Trail ends and you pick up the white blazes of the main Bruce Trail.

21. Turn left here on to the main Bruce Trail and follow it as it dips up and down. Climb over a stile and walk along the edge of a steep valley just below and then on top of the ridge.

22. After the stile there are several forks in the trail. Always stay left. About 1k after the stile, you come to The Quarryman's Side Trail. Turn left, following its blue blazes down the escarpment. The forest here is full of wildflowers, especially in the spring when the trilliums and jack-in-the-pulpit are in their glory.

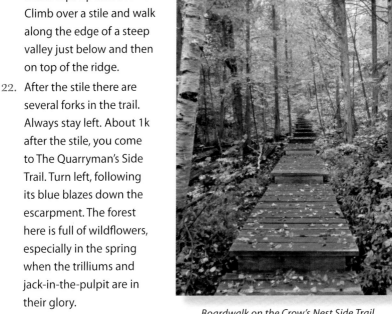

Boardwalk on the Crow's Nest Side Trail.

23. At the bottom of the hill, go straight past the washrooms across a lovely open valley – my favourite in all of Caledon. When I was a kid, we had an annual Thanksgiving Ride to this spot. Most of us would come on horseback. Meanwhile my dad and others had driven in and set up a huge cauldron that hung from a tripod over an open fire. Hot onion soup was on the menu along with crisp Macintosh apples. So stop here for a picnic while enjoying the rushing Credit River in a spot where the Oak Ridges Moraine cozies up to the Niagara Escarpment.

24. This is the end of The Quarryman's Side Trail. Pick up the white blazes of the main Bruce Trail heading generally to the left (downstream) as you look at the river.

25. The main Bruce Trail follows the old road that my dad used to transport that big cauldron. At one point the trail splits. Either route ends up at the same spot, so take your pick. Next you have a second chance to look at the lovely little houses in Brimstone as you retrace this portion of the route. Note some of their mailboxes and other creative house art.

26. As you leave the village, look up to your left. This was the site of the Big Hill Quarry. A two-inch steel cable used to hang high above the valley joining this quarry to the railway tracks near the "S" turn. A steam-operated aerial tram carried the quarried stone to the train station.

27. Stay on Dominion Street (the road through Brimstone) until you come to a stop sign. Turn right on to the Forks of the Credit Road, leaving the main Bruce Trail.

28. Retrace your earlier route under the trestle bridge. If you are lucky, Forks of the Credit honey will be on sale at the only house on the right side of the road. Turn left on to the Trimble Side Trail where it leaves the road at the base of the hill just after the bridge over the West Credit River.

29. Follow the Trimble Side Trail's blue blazes for about 600m, most of it uphill through a cedar forest, until you arrive back at the confluence of the Trimble and Crow's Nest side trails. This time, stay on the Trimble Side Trail, going straight ahead. DO NOT turn on to the Crow's Nest Side Trail.

30. Follow the Trimble Side Trail for about 1k until you come to a trail confluence. Follow The Gorge Loop into the Belfountain Conservation Area.

31. This gem of a park can be very busy on summer weekends. Only 8 hectares in size, it once belonged to Charles Mack, inventor of the cushion-back rubber stamp. Enjoy "Niagara Falls," "Yellowstone Cave" and the swinging bridge.

32. Leave the park through the main entrance and turn left on to the Forks of the Credit Road. Consider stopping at the Caledon Hills Ice Cream Parlour before heading up into the village proper where you will find a great coffee shop and a gift shop.

33. At the village stop sign, turn right on to Bush Street and pass by the landmark general store. Mostly shuttered in 2015, the store's role as a community meeting place is sorely missed by villagers.

34. Stay on Bush Street, possibly stopping in at Moorecroft's Antiques, until you arrive at Shaw's Creek Road.

35. Turn right and follow Shaw's Creek Road to River Road and your car.

Belfountain / Judy Charbonneau Loop

There is a steep set of rustic stairs on this hike. If you or your dog is not very agile, this might not be an ideal route.

OVERVIEW

The Forks of the Credit is among the most spectacular sections of the almost 900-kilometre-long Bruce Trail, and this loop takes you up the Devil's Pulpit on a climb of 120 vertical metres. It also passes through the hamlet of Belfountain where there is a café, the Belfountain Inn and, count 'em, two ice cream parlours. These amenities are added incentive for you to complete this challenging loop.

For over a decade, Judy Charbonneau owned and operated the Belfountain Village Store. During her tenure, it was the heart of the village. Judy was community-minded, a great hiker and dear friend who passed away in 2005.

Part way up the escarpment, you visit a hidden lime kiln ruin. In late June, look for yellow Lady's Slipper orchids near here. Farther up the trail there are rare walking ferns. A stroll along Caledon Mountain Drive, one of the most prestigious addresses in Ontario according to the *Toronto Star*, completes the loop. Check out the lovely homes. This route has it all: woods, views, estates, lattes, food and calorie-burning climbs.

*This route is generously sponsored by **The Friends of the Greenbelt Foundation** (**greenbelt.ca**).*

6

Nicola's
Insider Info

LENGTH
8.5 kilometres

LEVEL OF DIFFICULTY
Moderate

LENGTH OF TIME
2 to 3 hours

NUMBER OF STEPS
11,827

kCAL BURNED 393

HIGHLIGHTS
Exercise, Devil's Pulpit, view, Credit River, walking fern, lime kiln, Belfountain's Salamander Festival takes place the last Saturday in September.

PLACES TO EAT/DRINK
Higher Ground Coffee Co., Belfountain Inn, Caledon Hills Ice Cream Parlour

ENTRANCE FEE
n/a

GPS

TRAIL MARKER
Loop 6

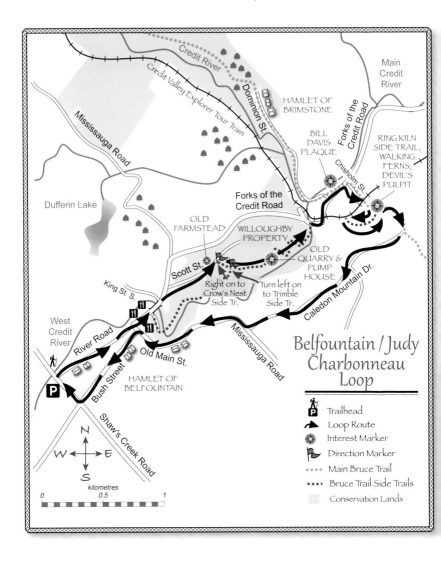

Belfountain / Judy Charbonneau Loop

Credit River
Credit Valley Explorer Tour Train
Mississauga Road
Dominion St.
HAMLET OF BRIMSTONE
Main Credit River
BILL DAVIS PLAQUE
Forks of the Credit Road
Chisholm St.
RING KILN SIDE TRAIL, WALKING FERNS, DEVIL'S PULPIT
Dufferin Lake
Forks of the Credit Road
OLD FARMSTEAD
WILLOUGHBY PROPERTY
OLD QUARRY & PUMP HOUSE
Scott St.
Right on to Crow's Nest Side Tr.
Turn left on to Trimble Side Tr.
Caledon Mountain Dr.
King St. S.
West Credit River
River Road
Bush Street
Old Main St.
HAMLET OF BELFOUNTAIN
Mississauga Road
Shaw's Creek Road

Legend:
- Trailhead
- Loop Route
- Interest Marker
- Direction Marker
- Main Bruce Trail
- Bruce Trail Side Trails
- Conservation Lands

N W E S

kilometres
0   0.5   1

"Everywhere is walking distance if you have the time."
STEVEN WRIGHT

Directions

(*As Caledon Hikes* went to press there was ongoing discussion about rerouting hikers to keep them off the gravel portion of Scott Street. Look for rerouting signs or check **www.nicolaross.ca** for a route change.)

1. Park on River Road where it meets Shaw's Creek Road just west of Belfountain.

2. Walk east along River Road toward Belfountain.

3. When you come to the stop sign where River Road meets Old Main Street in the village, walk straight ahead down the hill past the Belfountain Inn and the Belfountain Conservation Area.

4. Cross the bridge over the West Credit River and up out of the valley. At the top of the hill veer right (straight) on to Scott Street.

5. Follow Scott Street to the gate at #100. You are entering the Willoughby Property, which is a lovely piece of public land managed by Credit Valley Conservation. Pedestrians are welcome. This land was quarried in the late 1880s, well before Bert Willoughby, of Gibson Willoughby Real Estate, built an enormous house at the end of the road near the Forks of the Credit.

6. About 200m after the gate, the Crow's Nest Side Trail crosses the road. Veer right (straight) onto the trail, leaving the road and following the blue blazes of the Crow's Nest Side Trail.

7. Follow this trail for another 200m until you come to a confluence of the Crow's Nest Side Trail and the Trimble Side Trail. As you walk on the long boardwalk look for the trail junction.

8. Turn right leaving the Crow's Nest Side Trail and then almost immediately turn left on to the Trimble Side Trail. Roy and John Trimble came to Belfountain because their father bought what is now the coffee shop and gift store. At the time, it was a blacksmith's shop that the Trimble brothers turned into a gas station and mechanic shop when cars replaced horses. Roy was a great naturalist who knew the area well. The trail is named after Roy and his wife Eleanor.

9. Follow the blue blazes of the Trimble Side Trail as it makes its way through a cedar forest. You skirt the top of a cliff to your right. Along the way, there is a great lookout where you can gaze over the Credit River valley. This is especially beautiful in the spring as new leaves are forming and in the fall when the trees are alive with colour.

10. Heading steadily downhill, you pass by large mounds that are actually slag heaps of rubble left over from quarrying days.

11. You pass by a wooden pump house below on your right. Just past it, look back behind the pump house. See if you can make out the remains of a stone bridge. It once had train tracks over it. Trains were used to transport the enormous rocks from the quarries to the railway station that was situated at the "S" turn on the Forks of the Credit Road. My mum, now in her 90s, used to flag down the train at this station and take it into Toronto. Now the Credit Valley Explorer Tour train and freight trains use the tracks.

12. A few metres further along the trail look for a grove of rare blue-beech trees (*Carpinus caroliniana*). They are also known as musclewood trees because the smooth ridges on their trunks make them look like muscles and because blue-beech is very hard. It was used to make axe handles. The most noticeable one has been partly chopped down and overhangs the trail.

13. Look out for a sharp right-hand turn that goes down some stairs before the trail empties on to the Forks of the Credit Road at a bridge that passes over the gushing west Credit River.

14. Turn right, go over the bridge and follow the Forks of the Credit Road for 300m, passing under the high trestle bridge until you come to Dominion Street. Take a short detour to your left to the Dominion Street bridge and look upstream. You will see the west and main branches of the Credit River come together, thereby giving this area its name. The road is narrow as it goes under the trestle. Best to walk on the right side of the road where there is a shoulder.

15. Return to the Forks of the Credit Road and continue walking along it for another 250m until you come to Chisholm Street. Before you come to Chisholm Street look for a plaque on the river side of the road. Erected by The Friends of the Greenbelt Foundation, it honours former Premier William G. Davis for his efforts to balance urban areas with farming and the protection of important environmental features. Created in 2005, the Greenbelt added one million acres of farmland and environmentally sensitive areas to the already-protected Niagara Escarpment and Oak Ridges Moraine.

16. Turn right on to Chisholm Street by a cauldron planted with lovely flowers. You are on the main Bruce Trail with its white blazes.

The best view in Caledon.

17.   At the end of little Chisholm Street on the left behind a high fence is an old red brick schoolhouse where one of my sisters and my brother attended school in the 1950s and 1960s.

18.   The trail enters the forest and starts up a very steep incline. After 200m, and winded, you come out on to railway tracks. Cross them with care as there are trains, and re-enter the forest.

19.   Continue climbing for about 125m until you see the signs for the Ring Kiln Side Trail. Look out for some rails from old railway tracks that were once used to transport rocks from the quarries. There is very little left of these old spur lines. As I understand it, during WWII, every scrap of old metal was collected and reused as part of the war effort.

20.   Turn right and follow the Ring Kiln Side Trail with its blue blazes for 600m. It takes you to an amazing sight. When I first came across this lime kiln, I thought I was in the Guatemalan jungle looking at Mayan ruins. It's an extraordinary spot that is difficult to get to. There is an interpretive sign.

21. After exploring the lime kiln and, if you are there in late June, looking for yellow Lady's Slipper orchids, return to the main Bruce Trail retracing the trail you came in on.

22. When you reach the main Bruce Trail, turn right following the white blazes up hill.

23. Continue climbing through a rock garden in a dense cedar forest. Ice and snow are often present here into the summer months. Look for the rare walking fern, so called because it roots from the "tip" of its long slender leaves. This fern is only found on north-facing slopes of the escarpment and doesn't really look like a typical fern.

24. Keep climbing until you reach a sheer cliff and a set of crude stone stairs. Use the cable to make your way to the top of the escarpment. Look for fossils in the limestone as you go up.

25. At the top, look out over the valley. In the distance you can see an enormous lone house that was built by George Eaton of the Eaton's store Eatons. In autumn, this is the place to see the fall colours. Put on your shades, you are going to need them.

26. When you have caught your breath and had some water, continue on. In the spring, there are great trilliums in this area. Soon the trail comes to Caledon Mountain Drive. The Bruce Trail goes straight ahead, but you will turn right and walk along this paved road.

27. Follow Caledon Mountain Drive for about 1.5k, taking in some beautiful homes. At the end of Caledon Mountain Drive, turn right on to Mississauga Road. You may want to walk on the right side of the road where the shoulder is wider. Follow this rather busy bit of road for under 1k until you reach Belfountain and your reward of a latte or smoked salmon and cream cheese bagel.

28. At the village stop sign turn left on to Bush Street. Walk along Bush Street, perhaps stopping at Moorecroft's Antiques. Go up the hill to a stop sign at Shaw's Creek Road.

29. Turn right on to Shaw's Creek Road until you return to River Road and your vehicle.

Belfountain Luckenuf Loop

The Belfountain Conservation Area can be busy on weekends, making parking scarce. It's best to do this hike during the week or early on a weekend day.

OVERVIEW

The 8-hectare Belfountain Conservation Area was home to Charles Mack, inventor of the cushion-back rubber stamp. Charles and his wife Addie purchased the property in 1908 and developed it into a whimsical, Dr. Seuss-like place complete with "Niagara Falls" and "Yellowstone Cave." They called it Luckenuf.

This fun, short walk takes you by a water fountain (toss in a coin for good luck) that is capped by a bell, which is appropriate given it's in the Belfountain Conservation Area. From the suspension bridge, look over the falls as water crashes into a fern-filled canyon before the trail enters a forest and passes by remnants of an old limestone quarry. You drop down to the river where it gushes over rocks and is a cool place to be on a warm summer day. After crossing back over the river, you climb along a pretty trail until it comes out to one of Belfountain's hidden back streets. This picturesque route covers some hilly, rocky and occasionally slippery terrain.

"I dream of hiking into my old age."
MARLYN DOAN

Nicola's
Insider Info

LENGTH
3 kilometres

LEVEL OF DIFFICULTY
Moderate

LENGTH OF TIME
45 minutes to 1 hour

NUMBER OF STEPS
4,539

kCAL BURNED 149

HIGHLIGHTS
Swinging bridge, fountain, limestone slag heaps, Credit River, tufa, Belfountain's Salamander Festival takes place the last Saturday in September.

PLACES TO EAT/DRINK
Higher Ground Coffee Co., Belfountain Inn, Caledon Hills Ice Cream Parlour

ENTRANCE FEE
Adults $5/Children & Seniors $3

GPS

TRAIL MARKER
Loop 7

Directions

(*As* Caledon Hikes *went to press there was ongoing discussion about rerouting hikers to keep them off the gravel portion of Scott Street. Look for rerouting signs or check* **www.nicolaross.ca** *for a route change.*)

1. Park in the Belfountain Conservation Area where there are washrooms. Entrance Fee: Adults $5/Children & Seniors $3

2. Walk toward the kiosk that has a map of the Conservation Area.

3. Take the stairs behind the kiosk that lead down to the river.

4. At the bottom of the stairs go straight over the bridge, bypassing the Pond Loop Trail.

5. Turn right after crossing the bridge and follow the river. On your right there is an old grinding stone and a cement pond that has been filled in. When I was young, we swam in this protected pool, while the big kids braved the open river. Since then, silt has filled in behind the dam so it's no longer a swimming hole.

6. Walk past the stone fountain topped with a bell. It looks old, but was rebuilt in the 1990s by the grandson of the man who built the original fountain. Toss in a dime for good luck.

7. Turn right and cross the river on the suspension (swinging) bridge. Stop and have a look at the waterfalls built by the Macks as a mini Niagara Falls.

8. On the far side of the bridge, climb the wooden stairs and turn left following the Gorge Loop Trail.

9. After about 400m along this beautiful though rocky trail, you come to a wooden bridge that crosses back over the West Credit River. Along the way, look at the streams that cross the path. A beige-coloured material that looks like a cross between foam insulation and cement sometimes lines the streambed. This is tufa. Tufa is a natural, porous sedimentary rock consisting of calcium carbonate, the main component of lime. Tufa forms naturally in this area, explaining why there is a lime kiln ruin in the Forks of the Credit.

10. After crossing the bridge, you come to a trail junction where the Gorge Loop Trail goes left and the Trimble Side Trail goes right. Follow the blue blazes of the Trimble Side Trail to the right.

11. This trail leads you up out of the valley. You cross a makeshift, but well-worn path that heads to the river. Head down for another look at this pretty stream that is a magnet for those who like to fly fish. A little further up the

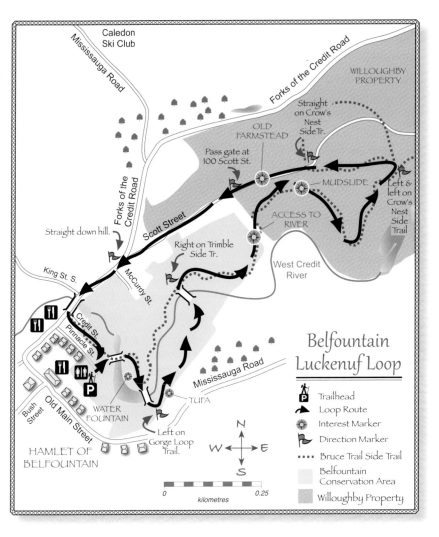

Belfountain
Luckenuf Loop

Caledon
Ski Club

Mississauga Road

Forks of the Credit Road

WILLOUGHBY
PROPERTY

Straight
on Crow's
Nest
Side Tr.

OLD
FARMSTEAD

Pass gate at
100 Scott St.

MUDSLIDE

Left &
left on
Crow's
Nest
Side
Trail

Forks of the
Credit Road

Scott Street

ACCESS TO
RIVER

Straight down hill.

Right on Trimble
Side Tr.

West Credit
River

King St. S.

McCurdy St.

Credit St.

Pinnacle St.

Mississauga Road

TUFA

Bush
Street

Old Main Street

P

WATER
FOUNTAIN

Left on
Gorge Loop
Trail.

HAMLET OF
BELFOUNTAIN

Belfountain
Luckenuf Loop

🚶 Trailhead
⚑ Loop Route
✺ Interest Marker
⚑ Direction Marker
•••• Bruce Trail Side Trail
  Belfountain
  Conservation Area
  Willoughby Property

N
W — E
S

0   0.25
kilometres

valley you walk along a boardwalk over an area where there is evidence of
the mudslide that obliterated the original path.

12. Follow the Trimble Side Trail until you come to a junction with the Crow's
Nest Side Trail. Turn left on the Crow's Nest Side Trail leaving the Trimble
Side Trail.

13. Follow the blue blazes for the Crow's Nest Side Trail up a few wooden steps
until you come to a sign that indicates the Crow's Nest Side Trail goes both
left and right. Go left on the boardwalk.

14. Walk along the boardwalk until it ends and becomes a footpath through a mature mixed forest. Look for shaggy-barked ironwood trees that are also known as hophornbeams (*Ostrya virginiana*). This part of the trail is home for me. I live in Belfountain and have walked this section a thousand times, mostly with my great canine companion Mota who passed away in May 2014, just short of her 16th birthday.

The Bell fountain.

15. A few minutes later, the trail comes to a small gravel road. This is Scott Street and you leave the Crow's Nest Side Trail here. Veer left (straight) on to Scott Street.

16. You are passing through the Willoughby Property. Owned by Ontario Heritage Trust and managed by Credit Valley Conservation, this public land was once the site of a number of active limestone quarries. The enormous, sometimes-pink rocks excavated here were often shipped to Toronto. Queen's Park and parts of the University of Toronto were made from Credit Valley limestone. Keep an eye out for the site of an old farmstead on your right. The big maples give it away.

17. Pass through a gate with Credit Valley signs where Scott Street becomes paved. Continue along this pleasant street that was once the main route between Belfountain and the Forks of the Credit. There was supposed to have once been a brothel along this stretch of road.

18. Scott Street meets the Forks of the Credit Road at a stop sign. Keep heading straight (left) on the Forks of the Credit Road down the hill.

19. At the bottom of the hill you cross over the Credit River and turn left on to Credit Street to re-enter the Belfountain Conservation Area. Or take this opportunity to have ice cream in the Caledon Hills Ice Cream Parlour next door.

Bolton Loop

With over 25,000 residents,
Bolton is Caledon's only "urban" centre.

OVERVIEW

This loop was a most welcome surprise. Angus and Sien Doughty, who live in Bolton and know all about the outdoors, described it to me. How wonderful that within Bolton's town limits, there is a 9.7k hike that is almost exclusively on trails.

For the most part, the route follows the Humber River, making great use of the Humber Valley Heritage Trail. But it also swings down into the old Bolton Camp, a large piece of land recently acquired by Toronto and Region Conservation Authority. Linking it together are some gorgeous trails through a series of ravines and the Sunkist Woods. The houses that back onto the wetlands just south of Colombia Way have very nice views that are rich with birdlife. I finished up the route at about 10:30am on a Sunday morning and, in great Caledon tradition, stopped for a latte at Archtop Café in Bolton. It was a sweet ending to a lovely hike.

This loop has a Moderate rating since there is lots of up and down. In general, however, the footing is excellent.

"One step at a time is good walking."
CHINESE PROVERB

Nicola's
Insider Info

LENGTH
9.7 kilometres

LEVEL OF DIFFICULTY
Moderate

LENGTH OF TIME
2.5 to 3.5 hours

NUMBER OF STEPS
13,358

kCAL BURNED
440

HIGHLIGHTS
Humber River, wetlands, rapids, ravines, all in Bolton

PLACES TO EAT/DRINK
Archtop Café and many, many more

ENTRANCE FEE
n/a

TRAIL MARKER
Loop 8

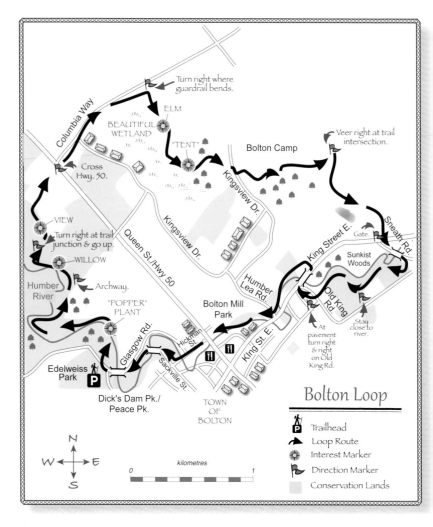

Directions

1. Park in the lot at Edelweiss Park on Glasgow Road in Bolton on the west side of Highway 50. Parking can be tight if there are soccer matches in progress. Another option is to park at Dick's Dam Park.

2. Cross Glasgow Road looking for the Humber Valley Heritage Trail sign. Take this well-trodden path. It is marked with white blazes.

3. Roughly following the Humber River, the trail goes into and out of forested areas. In between there are lots of what I call "popper plants" with seed

pods that explode when you pinch them. The experience is like popping plastic bubble wrap. The trail goes up and down into and out of the river valley. Look for a lovely weeping willow shade tree. You also pass under an archway made of sticks by some handy hikers before heading down some steps to the stream.

4. After about 2k you come to an obvious T-intersection. In 2014, there were no markers telling you which trail goes where. Take the right-hand trail. The other one goes on to Palgrave. The wide path goes up a steep incline. At the top, there is a nice view of the Humber Valley behind you.

5. About 800m after the trail junction, you come to traffic lights on Highway 50. Cross the highway at the lights and follow Columbia Way. There is a sidewalk on the south side of this, the only tedious section of the route.

6. After about 900m, the sidewalk turns to asphalt and the guardrail bends. Leave Columbia Way here, following an asphalt footpath that leaves the road and goes to the right.

7. The trail skirts a wetland, crosses another paved trail and then heads down into the wetland again. On your right, as you climb up, there is a graceful elm tree that has survived Dutch Elm disease. The disease hit Ontario with a vengeance in 1967 and I remember whole forests of dead trees. My dad cried when he had to cut down the beauty by our house. The disease was introduced to North America by a furniture company that imported infected wood. The European elm bark beetle was more effective at spreading the disease than our native elm bark beetle and soon an epidemic was underway. The website dutchelmdisease.ca states, "Sounds lofty to say, but think about it: Dutch elm disease has affected everything from the way we view monoculture street plantings to our understanding of invasive pests. It forever altered urban forestry policy and law, and certainly changed the public's awareness of street tree management."

8. The path arrives at Kingsview Drive (no street sign). Cross it, turn right and at the end of the guardrail turn left on a new trail that was unmarked in 2014. It heads down into property formerly called the Bolton Camp that was recently acquired by the Toronto and Region Conservation Authority, and will soon offer lots of hiking options.

9. This wide track meanders through a forest for 1.5k with only one obvious intersecting trail. When you come to the intersecting trail, veer right heading uphill and out of the forest.

CALEDON HIKES — *Loops & Lattes*

10. Follow what is now a grassy track across a field beside a big fenced-in pond and head down an incline that leads to a green metal gate. There were No Trespassing signs here but the Toronto and Region Conservation Authority said it was okay to walk the trail.

11. Climb over the gate and cross Old King Road WITH CAUTION. It's a busy street.

12. On the far side of Old King Road, turn left for a few metres until you come to little Sneath Road, which dekes off to the right. Follow it until it ends at a pedestrian trail that goes over a footbridge.

13. Immediately after crossing the footbridge, turn right on a footpath. You will see a signpost for the Humber Valley Heritage Trail (HVHTA) and some white blazes.

14. Follow the Humber Valley Heritage Trail, sticking close to the river. This section of trail was overgrown and poorly marked when I walked it. When in doubt, stay close to the river, which is on your right.

15. You pass through groves of staghorn sumac (*Rhus typhina*). The red flowers, whose shape give the plant its name, can be turned into lemonade and make a good dye.

16. Follow this trail for about 750m, going over a small wooden bridge that is marked by a white blaze. Then the blazes disappear. Don't panic, just stay on the trail and follow the river even when you come to trails that lead away from the Humber.

17. You will come to a green post with a white blaze. Walk past it until the trail ducks under some trees/bushes and you come to what was once a paved driveway. Turn right here for a short distance following the pavement until you arrive at Old King Road.

18. Turn right on Old King Road and cross King Street at the traffic lights.

19. Turn right on King Street, crossing over the bridge.

20. At the end of the bridge the Humber Valley Heritage Trail makes itself known again. Turn left and follow it along the river. The Humber picks up speed through this section and you may see small rapids.

21. This manicured trail follows the Humber River, passing through a parkette before arriving at Humber Lea Road. Cross Humber Lea Road and enter Bolton Mill Park. The river here was diverted for flood control after Bolton was badly damaged by Hurricane Hazel in 1955. Ontario's conservation

"Popper Plant" — as much fun as bubble wrap.

authorities are unique in Canada as they manage rivers from source to mouth. While it seems this would be the logical way to look after a river, it's not often done. The province's conservation authorities were mostly created around 1950 to deal with recurrent and often devastating flooding.

22. When you come to Highway 50 take the underpass. Pick up Hickman Street on the west side of Highway 50 and follow it to Sackville Street.

23. Turn right on Sackville Street. At the dead end, turn left following the white blazes of the Humber Valley Heritage Trail, which have reappeared.

24. Follow the white blazes through Dick's Dam Park, over a bridge and into Peace Park.

25. When you see the big stone surrounded by flagpoles that says Peace Park (ahead of you, but off to your left), turn right, leaving the park and exiting on to Glasgow Road.

26. Pass over the old Stratford Bridge Co. metal bridge – that I notice is a heritage structure – and follow Glasgow Road back to Edelweiss Park and your car.

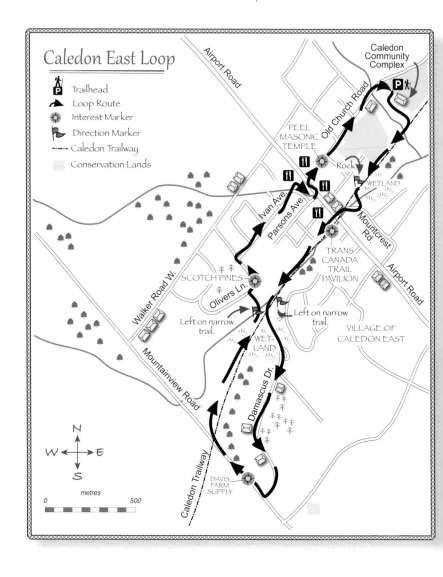

Caledon East Loop

- Trailhead
- Loop Route
- Interest Marker
- Direction Marker
- Caledon Trailway
- Conservation Lands

Airport Road

Caledon Community Complex

Old Church Road

PEEL MASONIC TEMPLE

Rock

WETLAND

Ivan Ave.

Parsons Ave.

Mountcrest Rd.

Airport Road

TRANS CANADA TRAIL PAVILION

Walker Road W.

SCOTCH PINES

Olivers Ln.

Left on narrow trail.

Left on narrow trail.

VILLAGE OF CALEDON EAST

Mountainview Road

WET-LAND

Damascus Dr.

N
W — E
S

metres
0   500

Caledon Trailway

DAVIS FARM SUPPLY

Walking is the exact balance between spirit and humility."
GARY SNYDER

Caledon East Loop

OVERVIEW

Caledon East is the geographic centre of the Town of Caledon. It is also the seat of our local government and home to the courthouse, main police station, many soccer pitches and dual ice rinks. As a result, this small town has more amenities than you'd expect, including a liquor store, fabulous butcher, fine pastry shops, cafés and several restaurants.

This short hike will help you get to know Caledon's "capital town." Beginning on the Caledon Trailway, which is part of the Trans Canada Trail, it passes by the first pavilion built on this ambitious cross-country project. You can stop and read the names of those who have contributed to the trail and while you are there look at the stones laid to honour Caledon residents who were international stars. The Walk of Fame pays tribute to Farley Mowat, Elmer Iseler and Norman Jewison, among others.

The route passes through an upscale rural subdivision, which Caledon seems to have lots of, before taking you back to the Trailway and into the village proper. When you pass between Gabe's Country Bake Shoppe and the Caledon Hills Coffee Company, you'll have to decide which will tickle your fancy more.

Nicola's Insider Info

LENGTH
5.7 kilometres

LEVEL OF DIFFICULTY
Easy

LENGTH OF TIME
1.5 to 2 hours

NUMBER OF STEPS
7,988

kCAL BURNED 246

HIGHLIGHTS
Trans Canada Trail Pavilion, Caledon Walk of Fame, Caledon Environmentalists of the Year, Masonic Temple, churches, Davis Farm Supply

PLACES TO EAT/DRINK
Gabe's Country Bake Shoppe, Caledon Hills Coffee Company, Gourmandissimo, Prime Beef Bistro and more

ENTRANCE FEE
n/a

TRAIL MARKER
Loop 9

Directions

1. Park in the lot at the Caledon Community Complex on Old Church Road east of Airport Road.

2. Walk on the right-hand side of the Complex heading away from Old Church Road.

3. Behind the building pick up a worn, though unmarked, trail that goes past a gazebo en route to the Caledon Trailway, which parallels Old Church Road.

4. Turn right on to the Caledon Trailway.

5. When you arrive at a large rock on the left side of the trail with a plaque recognizing Caledon's environmental leaders, turn left onto the boardwalk over the wetland. Caledon was once voted the greenest town in Ontario and that designation is due in large part because of the individuals listed on this plaque. (I'm proud to say my name appeared in 2004.)

6. Follow the boardwalk to its end and turn right on to a paved subdivision road (Mountcrest Rd.).

7. Shortly, you arrive at busy Airport Road. Turn right on to Airport Road, go a few metres and then cross it at the Caledon Trailway crosswalk. Obey the lights on this busy highway.

8. Once across Airport Road, stay on the Caledon Trailway. Very soon you will see a clearing on your left. Stop by the Trans Canada Trail Pavilion here. It was the first built on this ambitious project and bears the names of those who have donated money to it. Right beside the pavilion is the Caledon Walk of Fame. It consists of large flat stones that form a walkway with each stone bearing the name of a well-known person who once called Caledon home, including Farley Mowat, Norman Jewison, Elmer Iseler and others.

9. Return to the Trailway and keep heading west until you come to a worn, though narrower, trail that crosses the Trailway at right angles. It is about 700m from Airport Road. Turn left on this unmarked path.

10. Follow it through the wetland and up a gentle slope that leads into a rural subdivision consisting of enormous lots and relatively modest homes. At least the houses seem dwarfed by the size of the lots and the tall, mostly coniferous trees that separate them.

11. Follow Damascus Drive for almost a kilometre until it ends at Mountainview Road. As you near Mountainview Road, gaze across the farmer's field on the

west side. The contrast of the flat agricultural field against Caledon's rising hills is striking.

Caledon's Walk of Fame.

12. Turn right on to Mountainview Road. This paved road is a bit busy, so stay on the shoulder. You may want to pick up some fresh vegetables at Davis Farm Supply if it's open.

13. After less than a half kilometre, you leave the road and turn right on to the Caledon Trailway.

14. Follow the Trailway for about 700m until you return to the same narrower unmarked path that you took earlier. This time turn left on this trail.

15. Follow this path through a reforested alley that is fenced on both sides. It leads into another subdivision. Turn right on Olivers Lane, the first road you come to. Look for some beautiful Scotch pines that soar overhead. Their trunks are a coppery colour.

16. At Ivan Avenue turn right.

17. Ivan Avenue turns right and dead-ends at Parsons Avenue.

18. Turn left on to Parsons Avenue and follow it until it hits Airport Road.

19. Now you have to decide: Will it be Gabe's Country Bake Shoppe, Caledon Hills Coffee Company or maybe pizza?

20. When your stomach is sated, follow Airport Road to the traffic lights at Old Church Road.

21. Cross to the east side and follow Old Church Road for about 700m until you return to the Caledon Community Complex on the right side of the road where you parked your car. There are a couple of churches along this stretch of the appropriately named Old Church Road, as well as the Peel Masonic temple tucked back on the north side of the road.

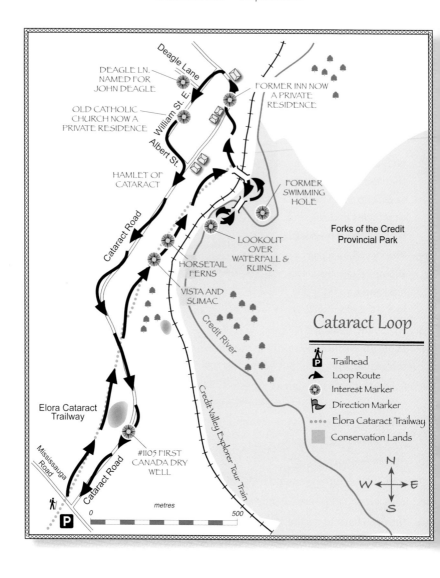

DEAGLE LN. NAMED FOR JOHN DEAGLE

Deagle Lane

FORMER INN NOW A PRIVATE RESIDENCE

OLD CATHOLIC CHURCH NOW A PRIVATE RESIDENCE

William St. E.

Albert St.

HAMLET OF CATARACT

FORMER SWIMMING HOLE

Forks of the Credit Provincial Park

Cataract Road

LOOKOUT OVER WATERFALL & RUINS.

HORSETAIL FERNS

VISTA AND SUMAC

Credit River

Cataract Loop

Trailhead

Loop Route

Interest Marker

Direction Marker

Elora Cataract Trailway

Conservation Lands

Elora Cataract Trailway

Credit Valley Explorer Tour Train

Mississauga Road

Cataract Road

#1105 FIRST CANADA DRY WELL

N
W — E
S

metres

0   500

P

"I have two doctors, my left leg and my right."

G.M. TREVELYAN

Cataract Loop

There is a spot along this loop that can be very wet in spring.

OVERVIEW

If you have houseguests who are up for a local-lore-filled stroll, this loop is for you. In about an hour, you will see the cascading waterfall that gives the hamlet of Cataract its name, ruins of the old Cataract Electric Co., a lovely Catholic Church and a once-famous, sometimes-infamous, wayside inn. Built before 1870, the brick Cataract Inn didn't need to be at the junction of Credit Valley Railway's mainline to Orangeville and its branch line to Elora to do a healthy business. Industrial development was so robust, Cataract supported two inns and two boardinghouses.

Operated by Mrs. William Glen as the Dewdrop Inn from 1880 until 1916, it was a busy place where workers from local quarries and mills as well as passengers from eight daily trains quenched their thirst. When Cataract's boom ebbed, Mrs. Glen sold her inn to Mary and Kate McEnaney. Members of a prominent Cataract family, the sisters turned the Dewdrop into a store and post office. It wasn't that the McEnaneys were teetotalers; it was just that the family already owned the village's other hotel, the Junction House.

Directions

1. Park on Mississauga Road where it meets Cataract Road and the Elora Cataract Trailway south of Charleston Side Road.

2. Walk east on the Elora Cataract Trailway.

3. Stay on the Trailway as it crosses Cataract Road and enters the Forks of the Credit Provincial Park. As you walk along the path look your right for vistas across the Credit River valley. There are some fine sumac trees to your left. They seem to attract robins in the spring. Also keep an eye out for horsetail ferns that look like miniature bamboo.

4. About 750m from where you crossed Cataract Road, you come to an intersection of trails. Turn right here and follow the path down to a metal bridge that goes over a set of railway tracks. This is the old Credit Valley Railway line once used by steam trains. Today, freight trains and the Credit Valley Explorer Tour train use these tracks. The latter takes paying customers on a great trip from Orangeville to Streetsville passing through the Forks of the Credit and travelling over the high trestle bridge en route. The Elora Cataract Trailway was the Credit Valley Railway's branch line that terminated here.

5. At the end of the bridge, turn right following the Ruins Trail and go down a short hill to another metal bridge.

6. This bridge goes over the Credit River where there was once a dam. Built as part of the power plant, it created a great swimming hole for local residents.

7. Continue along the Ruins Trail until you come to a platform that gives you a view of a large waterfall. Above it are the remains of the Cataract Electric Co., built by John Deagle in the late 1800s. It once supplied power to nearby towns. After a flood damaged the facility, Deagle sold it to Ontario Hydro who decommissioned the plant and destroyed the dam – and Cataract's swimming hole. This waterfall took the life of several of my schoolmates and injured others who were foolish enough to tempt fate. So beware.

8. Return following the same route you've just come along, crossing the bridge over the former dam and going up the short rise. At the top of the rise, turn left and cross the bridge over the railway tracks.

9. At the Elora Cataract Trailway turn right (rather than left from where you came). The trail heads around a curve and up a gentle slope to Cataract Road where you leave the Forks of the Credit Park.

10. Turn right on to Cataract Road.

11. At the next corner, you see the beautifully restored, red brick Cataract Inn. For a time, it was operated as a restaurant by this name. For many years before that, it was the Horseshoe Inn and people used to bring their bottles of wine in brown paper bags. A Georgian structure, built around 1870, it opened as the Cataract Junction and did well serving food, alcoholic beverages and, some say, fine women until the temperance movement put an end to these activities. For more stories about this inn (now a private residence) see the Overview on page 65.

Cataract Electric Co. ruins.
PHOTO BY NICK MARSHALL

12. Follow the road around the left-turning corner past the inn. Turn left on to William Street E.

13. On your right look for Deagle Lane, named after the Cataract Electric Co. owner John Deagle. A little further on, also on your right, is an old brick Catholic Church that has been converted into a private residence.

14. William Street E turns left and becomes Albert Street before it dead-ends at Cataract Road.

15. Turn right on to Cataract Road and follow it through the hamlet and past the Elora Cataract Trailway.

16. At #1105, you might see Crystal Springs'© tanker trucks carrying away water. The company reportedly still uses a well that was the first one used to make Canada Dry©, the "Champagne of Ginger Ales."

17. Continue along Cataract Road until you come to Mississauga Road and your car.

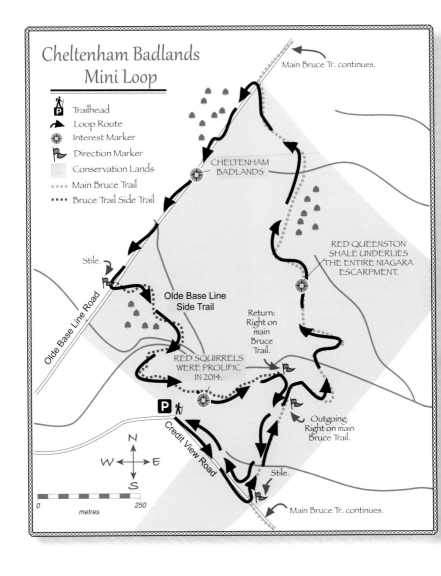

Cheltenham Badlands Mini Loop

- **P** Trailhead
- **➤** Loop Route
- **✳** Interest Marker
- **⚑** Direction Marker
- Conservation Lands
- •••• Main Bruce Trail
- ■■■■ Bruce Trail Side Trail

Main Bruce Tr. continues.

CHELTENHAM BADLANDS

RED QUEENSTON SHALE UNDERLIES THE ENTIRE NIAGARA ESCARPMENT.

Stile.

Olde Base Line Side Trail

Olde Base Line Road

Return: Right on main Bruce Trail.

RED SQUIRRELS WERE PROLIFIC IN 2014.

Outgoing: Right on main Bruce Trail.

Credit View Road

Stile.

Main Bruce Tr. continues.

N
W ← → E
S

0   metres   250

*"But the beauty is in the walking —
we are betrayed by destinations."*

GWYN THOMAS

Cheltenham Badlands Mini Loop

OVERVIEW

The Cheltenham Badlands are the highlight of this two-bite-brownie of a route. And like those delicious chocolate morsels, it is a sweet little thing. The loop takes you through some regenerating forest where the proliferation of apple and thorn trees gives away the fact that cattle used to graze here. You drop into a valley, cross a stream and climb gently up until you arrive at the Cheltenham Badlands. Allow enough time to take in these strangely hypnotic red clay hills before heading back to your car via a different pathway. Without a stop at the badlands it's a quick 45-minute walk.

Tempting as it may be to explore all the crevasses, too many visitors is a growing problem for the badlands. Created as a result of erosion caused by overgrazing, the badlands now suffer from overuse by cellphone-toting tourists. Social media sites overflow with photos of these red clay hills, bringing yet more cellphone-toting tourists. Expect a crowd swarming over them if you are there on a warm weekend, but be a good citizen conservationist: sit back and enjoy them from afar.

11

Nicola's
Insider Info

LENGTH
3.3 kilometres

LEVEL OF DIFFICULTY
Easy

LENGTH OF TIME
45 minutes to 1 hour

NUMBER OF STEPS
4,562

kCAL BURNED 142

HIGHLIGHTS
Cheltenham Badlands

PLACES TO EAT/DRINK
Nowhere en route, but the nearby Cheltenham General Store has the biggest ice cream cones around.

ENTRANCE FEE
n/a

GPS

TRAIL MARKER
Loop 11

Directions

1. Park on Credit View Road just south of Olde Base Line Road where the shoulder has been expanded to allow for parking.

2. Walk south on Credit View Road for 250m until you come to the Bruce Trail sign on the right side of the road and a stile on the left.

3. Turn left and climb over the stile following the main Bruce Trail's white blazes.

4. After 300m you come to a fork. Take the right fork, continuing to follow the white blazes.

5. Continue for just over 1k until you pop out on to Olde Base Line Road.

6. Turn left on to Olde Base Line Road, watching for traffic since this is a busy paved road with lots of tourist traffic.

7. You almost immediately find yourself at the entrance to the Cheltenham Badlands, one of Caledon's most popular tourist sites. Russell Cooper, a photographer for the *Toronto Telegram*, owned the property for years. He once told me about the day he stopped by to question a couple who were having their wedding photos shot on the site. "Who gave you permission to use this property?" he asked politely. When the groom assured him the owner had, Cooper gave the couple the boot. He'd be mighty surprised to see the number of tourists drawn to his property by the plethora of photos that flood social media sites. He'd also be dismayed at the damage they do. So enjoy this amazing place, but please help preserve it by not walking on it. Be a citizen conservationist.

8. When ready to head back to your car, leave the badlands, turn left and continue west along Olde Base Line Road. Again, be very careful on this hilly road overrun by rubbernecking tourists.

9. After 300m, at the top of the next hill, you come to another stile and a sign for the Olde Base Line Side Trail. Turn left, climb over the stile and follow the blue blazes. I saw a number of red squirrels (*Tamiasciurus hudsonicus*) in this area (and elsewhere in Caledon). If you see piles of cores from pinecones, it's likely this member of the rodent family is about. Opportunistic, red squirrels also eat mice and chipmunks!

10. This path dips down into a valley and then climbs gently up the other side.

11. Soon you return to the first stile. Climb it and then turn right on to Credit View Road. Your car is up ahead.

Cheltenham Badlands, worth preserving.

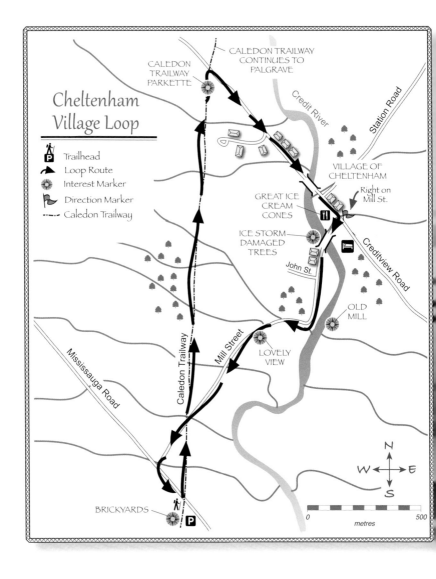

Cheltenham Village Loop

Legend:
- 🚶 Trailhead
- ➤ Loop Route
- ✹ Interest Marker
- ⚑ Direction Marker
- ·—·—· Caledon Trailway

CALEDON TRAILWAY CONTINUES TO PALGRAVE

CALEDON TRAILWAY PARKETTE

Credit River

Station Road

VILLAGE OF CHELTENHAM

GREAT ICE CREAM CONES

Right on Mill St.

ICE STORM DAMAGED TREES

John St.

Creditview Road

OLD MILL

LOVELY VIEW

Caledon Trailway

Mill Street

Mississauga Road

BRICKYARDS

N
W · E
S

0   metres   500

"An early-morning walk is a blessing for the whole day."

HENRY DAVID THOREAU

Cheltenham Village Loop

Nicola's Insider Info

LENGTH
4.5 kilometres

LEVEL OF DIFFICULTY
Easy

LENGTH OF TIME
1 to 1.5 hours

NUMBER OF STEPS
6,250

kCAL BURNED 203

HIGHLIGHTS
Cheltenham Brickyards, Cheltenham mill, ice cream at the Cheltenham General Store, Cheltenham Day is the first Saturday in July.

PLACES TO EAT/DRINK
Cheltenham General Store. There is also the Top of the Hill B&B in Cheltenham.

ENTRANCE FEE
n/a

GPS

TRAIL MARKER
Loop 12

OVERVIEW

This delightful, flat loop explores the picturesque village of Cheltenham and its environs. It starts at the historic brickyards on Mississauga Road. They were used for the filming of Timothy Findley's *The Wars*, and the buildings would have been destroyed if the Ontario Government had had its way. When the Town of Caledon sold the property to the province to offset the cost of building its municipal office in Caledon East, the province announced it was flattening the historic site. The Town stopped the demolition, but plans to develop a tourist train to run along tracks nearby (now the Caledon Trailway) never happened. In fact, the province sold the property to Brampton Brick Ltd., which has been removing the red clay for years. The company was obligated to preserve the buildings that once produced 90,000 bricks per day.

There is a lot to see on this relatively short, mostly flat loop, including Cheltenham's old mill and a lovely stretch of the Credit River. Along the way, stop in at the Cheltenham General Store for the best, aka biggest, ice cream cones around.

Directions

1. Park in the designated lot on the west side of Mississauga Road at the Caledon Trailway and the old brickyards, south of Olde Base Line Road.

2. The brickyards are a well-known landmark. The Interprovincial Brick Company produced the first bricks there in 1914. Carmen Delutis, who worked there from 1922 until the early 1960s, said that during WWII he was in charge of as many as 25 German prisoners of war. "They got paid – not full scale. They were good workers and we never thought they would try to escape," he recalls. At one point, the Interprovincial Brick Company produced 90,000 bricks a day from seven kilns. The Westminster Hospital in London, Ontario and the Skyline Hotel in Toronto were constructed from these bricks. Taken over by Domtar Inc. in 1928, the kilns operated until 1964 when pressed bricks replaced wire-cut ones.

3. Chinguacousy Township bought the land and buildings in 1972. The Town of Caledon took them over in 1974 and planned a park. The Town even moved a railway turnstile there so a steam train could use the old Hamilton & Northwestern Railway line. In 1975, however, the Town sold the land to the Ontario Government to offset the cost of building its municipal offices in Caledon East. In 1977, the Town successfully blocked provincial plans to demolish the old buildings. Unable to knock them down, the province invited private companies to build a brick-making plant. Cheltenham residents fought the application until, after a drawn-out fight, the company gave up its plans. But the citizens' victory was short-lived. They were shocked when the company came back with a new application. This time it succeeded in obtaining a license to remove some of the 35-million tonnes of red clay that lies under the property. For this reason, instead of being a park and terminal for the Credit Valley Steam Train, the old brickyards are attached to a mining operation. To obtain its license, the company agreed to preserve the historic buildings, protect environmentally sensitive areas and rehabilitate the quarries.

4. Carefully cross Mississauga Road and walk east along the Caledon Trailway. Stay on the Trailway after it crosses Mill Street. The trail is wide and flat with a cinder surface. As you follow the old Hamilton & Northwestern Railway route, you will pass through hardwood forests interspersed by farm fields, many still in agricultural production. Hay, corn and soybeans are the crops you are most likely to see. Note how hard they worked to fill in the deep ravines to keep

the grade flat on this rail bed. I spied a scarlet tanager when I walked this path, so keep your eyes peeled.

Cheltenham brickyards.

5. After about 2k you arrive at a small parkette and Credit View Road. Turn right on to Credit View Road, heading down for about 1k into the village of Cheltenham. There are a few lovely old stone and brick homes amid the newer ones. Cross over the Credit River on a wide bridge. I paddleboarded from Inglewood to Terra Cotta on the Credit River in 2014. Passing through Cheltenham where the river broadens was a peaceful part of this fabulous trip. Hopefully, the Caledon Hills Cycling shop in Inglewood will be guiding this trip in the future.

6. Stop in at the Cheltenham General Store for a coffee, snack or sandwich. Their ice cream cones are the most generous around.

7. Continue south on Credit View Road until you come to Mill Street at the base of the hill. Turn right on to Mill Street.

8. Cross the Credit River again at a spot where trees were badly damaged by the ice storm in 2013. Some enormous ones had to be cut down as a result.

9. Mill Street is a quiet road that parallels the Credit River for a time. There is a great vegetable garden in the flood plain on your left. Where the street turns sharp right look through the trees to see if you can make out the old Cheltenham mill on the other side of the Credit River. There are remains of an old dam there too. When we paddleboarded, this was the only spot where we had to pull our boards on shore and go around an obstacle.

10. Stay on Mill Street as it curves and climbs out of the valley. At the top of the rise, there is a lovely vista to the left over some farm fields. Keep walking on Mill Street until you come to Mississauga Road.

11. Turn left on to Mississauga Road until you come to the Caledon Trailway. Turn right and carefully cross Mississauga Road since cars roar along here. Your car should be waiting in the parking lot.

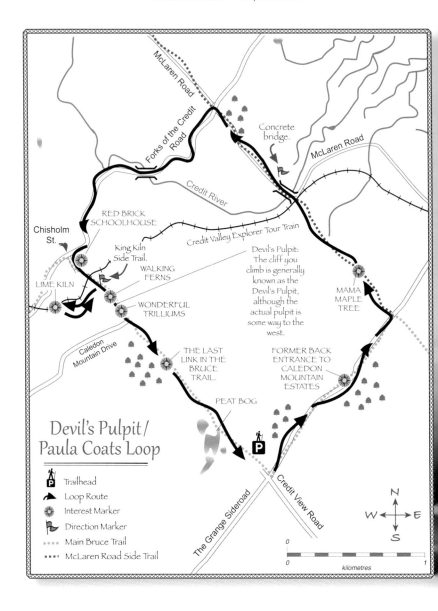

McLaren Road

Concrete bridge.

McLaren Road

Forks of the Credit Road

Credit River

RED BRICK SCHOOLHOUSE

Chisholm St.

King Kiln Side Trail.

Credit Valley Explorer Tour Train

Devil's Pulpit: The cliff you climb is generally known as the Devil's Pulpit, although the actual pulpit is some way to the west.

MAMA MAPLE TREE

LIME KILN

WALKING FERNS

WONDERFUL TRILLIUMS

Caledon Mountain Drive

THE LAST LINK IN THE BRUCE TRAIL.

FORMER BACK ENTRANCE TO CALEDON MOUNTAIN ESTATES

PEAT BOG

Devil's Pulpit/ Paula Coats Loop

🅿 Trailhead

➤ Loop Route

✹ Interest Marker

⚑ Direction Marker

···· Main Bruce Trail

---- McLaren Road Side Trail

The Grange Sideroad

Credit View Road

N
W — E
S

0
0 _____ 1
kilometres

"If you want to know if your brain is flabby, feel your legs."

BRUCE BARTON

Devil's Pulpit /
Paula Coats Loop

OVERVIEW

This is a great Thanksgiving Day loop. Put the turkey in the oven and head off for this rigorous hike. For two hours or more, you will climb up and down the Niagara Escarpment. When done, you will be home in time to prepare potatoes and vegetables before sitting down to a sumptuous, well-deserved meal. You might even tuck into an extra piece of pie.

The route takes you down the Niagara Escarpment, along the Forks of the Credit Road and then back up the escarpment via the Devil's Pulpit – even though it isn't the actual Devil's Pulpit. There is a side trip into the Mayan-like ruins of a lime kiln.

When you get back to the top of the escarpment, having climbed the last bit with the aid of a cable, look out over the best view in Caledon. Across the broad Credit River valley, look for a lone house, a mansion really, that was built by George Eaton of the Eaton's store Eatons.

In late September and the first half of October, this is the place to be to see the fall colours. Put on your shades, you are going to need them.

*This route is generously sponsored by **Caledon Hills Cycling** in Inglewood (**caledonhillscycling.com**).*

Nicola's
Insider Info

LENGTH
8 kilometres

LEVEL OF DIFFICULTY
Challenging

LENGTH OF TIME
2 to 3 hours

NUMBER OF STEPS
11,390

kCAL BURNED 375

HIGHLIGHTS
Devil's Pulpit view, lime kiln, mama maple, cardio, walking ferns, yellow Lady's Slipper

PLACES TO EAT/DRINK
No restaurants or stores on this route. In nearby Belfountain choose from the Higher Ground Coffee Co., Belfountain Inn, Caledon Hills Ice Cream Parlour.

ENTRANCE FEE
n/a

TRAIL MARKER
Loop 13

Directions

1. Park on Credit View Road on the north side of The Grange Side Road.

2. Turn left on to The Grange Side Road following the white blazes of the main Bruce Trail.

3. Follow this road for about 1.5k until you come to the top of a long steep downhill. Along the way, you pass what was once the back entrance to the Caledon Mountain Estates. Look for an old wire gate with a "Keep Gate Closed" sign on it. The other entrance is just south of Belfountain. The Eaton family purchased this large tract of land when the developer lost a battle to develop the second phase of the Caledon Mountain Estates.

4. You pass a blue sign wishing you a good day and then come to a set of yellow gates that close the road in the winter. As the road descends steeply, the main Bruce Trail turns right and enters the forest. DO NOT follow it. Instead, look for the blue sign for the McLaren Side Trail.

5. Follow the McLaren Side Trail and its blue blazes as it turns left into the forest. Soon you will emerge from the forest and see a great vista off to your right. Then the trail drops into an older-growth forest. There is a big mama maple to your right.

6. Together with her husband Don, Paula Coats led a weekly hike often along this route. Paula, who passed away suddenly in 2015, will be sorely missed by her hiking mates.

7. Continue down until the trail comes to the railway tracks. Both freight trains and the Credit Valley Explorer Tour train (www.creditvalleyexplorer.com) use these tracks. They were once the Credit Valley Railway that ran from Streetsville to Orangeville. It's a spectacular train trip over the trestle bridge in the Forks of the Credit.

8. Cross the tracks and follow the trail until it meets McLaren Road at a single-lane concrete bridge. I have a wonderful painting of this bridge by Julian Mulock, who painted the cover of *Caledon Hikes*. There is talk of replacing this bridge.

9. Keep following blue blazes over the bridge under which flows the Credit River. There was once a trout hatchery just past the bridge and you are not far from the grand Caledon Mountain Trout Club.

10. When you come to the Forks of the Credit Road turn left, leaving the McLaren Road Side Trail.

The rare walking fern.

11. Follow the Forks of the Credit Road. Take care on this beautiful winding road since there are several blind curves, and traffic on weekends can be busy. On blind corners consider crossing and walking on the right side of the road. Pass by the old ice cream shop and skirt the river. Look up to your left at the soaring cliffs of the Niagara Escarpment. This valley is brilliant in late September and early October as the red-coloured maples, orangey-brown beeches, white birches and evergreens put on a display.

12. Walk about 1.5k along the Forks of the Credit Road until you come to Chisholm Street. Turn left on to Chisholm Street passing by a cauldron planted with lovely flowers. You are now back on the main Bruce Trail with its white blazes.

13. At the end of little Chisholm Street behind a high fence on your left there is an old red brick schoolhouse where my sisters and brother attended school in the 1950s and 1960s.

14. The trail enters the forest and starts up a very steep incline. After about 200m climbing rustic steps, you come to the railway tracks again. Cross them and climb back into the forest.

15. Climb for about 125m more keeping a lookout for the Ring Kiln Side Trail.

16. Turn right on the Ring Kiln Side Trail following the blue blazes for 600m down to an amazing sight. When I first came across this lime kiln, I thought I was in the Guatemalan jungle looking at Mayan ruins. It's an extraordinary spot and well worth the in-and-out, calorie-burning trip.

17. After exploring the lime kiln (look for interpretive signs) return to the main Bruce Trail following the trail you just came in on. (If you visit the lime kiln in late June, look for large yellow Lady's Slipper orchids.)

18. When you reach the main Bruce Trail, turn right following the white blazes uphill.

19. Continue climbing through an amazing rock garden in a dense cedar forest. Look for the rare walking fern, so called because its tips root from the end of its long slender leaves. This fern is only found on north facing slopes on the escarpment and doesn't really look like a fern.

20. Keep climbing until you reach the base of a sheer cliff where a set of crude stone stairs provides a route up. Use the cable to make your way to the top of the escarpment.

21. At the top, take in the view. In the distance there is a lone house. It was built by George Eaton of the Eaton's store Eatons. On Thanksgiving weekend, there is no better place to see the fall colours.

22. Catch your breath, have some water and continue on the path. In the spring, there are great trilliums in this area. Soon the trail comes to Caledon Mountain Drive. This is where the road from The Grange Side Road would have arrived had the second phase of this development proceeded.

23. Stay straight following the white blazes of the main Bruce Trail.

24. This is a lovely rolling path that travels though a typical upland forest of maple, basswood and ash trees. Follow what becomes a broader track – it is the unopened road allowance for Credit View Road. This was the last link in the Bruce Trail. The trail builders were having trouble finding a route down the escarpment until they realized there was a road allowance here. Not only was it open to public use, it also descended the escarpment at one of the least steep places.

25. After about 1.4k, the trail goes by a green gate and past a driveway on the right. Up ahead is your car.

Duffy's Lane / Albion Hills Loop

Nicola's Insider Info

LENGTH
8.0 kilometres

LEVEL OF DIFFICULTY
Easy

LENGTH OF TIME
2 to 3 hours

NUMBER OF STEPS
11,046

kCAL BURNED 364

HIGHLIGHTS
Octagonal House,
Mill Lane, elms

PLACES TO EAT/DRINK
Nothing en route, but
both Caledon East and
Palgrave are nearby.

ENTRANCE FEE
Adult $6.50/Seniors
$5.50/<14 free

GPS

TRAIL MARKER
Loop 14

OVERVIEW

I am particularly pleased to include a walk along Mill Lane on this easy, flat loop. I came across this narrow winding street by accident and when I realized that by taking a little jaunt along the Caledon Trailway, I could include it, I added the extra distance. The route makes use of the trails in the Albion Hills Conservation Area and much of it is on the Humber Valley Heritage Trail. It takes you through forests and farms and at one particular spot you are requested to keep your dog on leash since there are sheep nearby.

The last bit is along busy Old Church Road, but it's a short distance and worth the unpleasantness in order to have over seven great kilometres of trails and country lanes. Besides, Old Church Road is worth noting since it once featured five churches. I can think of only two now, but you will see an octagonal house along it as well.

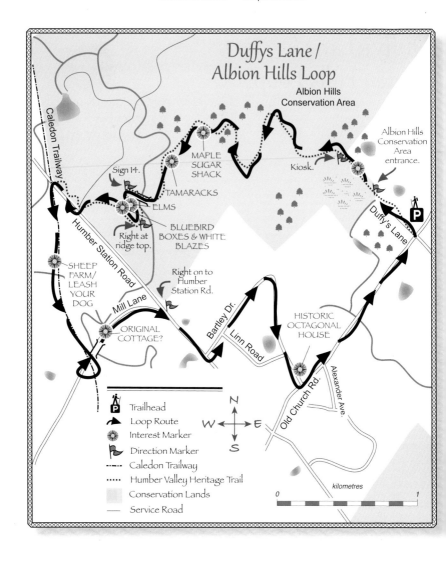

Duffys Lane / Albion Hills Loop

Albion Hills Conservation Area

Albion Hills Conservation Area entrance.

Caledon Trailway

Sign 14.

MAPLE SUGAR SHACK

Kiosk.

TAMARACKS

ELMS

Right at ridge top.

BLUEBIRD BOXES & WHITE BLAZES

Humber Station Road

SHEEP FARM / LEASH YOUR DOG

Right on to Humber Station Rd.

Mill Lane

ORIGINAL COTTAGE?

Bartley Dr.

Linn Road

Duffy's Lane

HISTORIC OCTAGONAL HOUSE

Old Church Rd.

Alexander Ave.

Legend:

- ▐P Trailhead
- ➤ Loop Route
- ✺ Interest Marker
- ⚑ Direction Marker
- ·—·— Caledon Trailway
- ······ Humber Valley Heritage Trail
- Conservation Lands
- —— Service Road

N
W   E
S

kilometres
0   1

*"If I could not walk far and fast,
I think I should just explode and perish."*

CHARLES DICKENS

Directions

1. Park on Duffy's Lane where it forms a dead end just north of Old Church Road.

2. Head north on the well-marked Humber Valley Heritage Trail. Like the main Bruce Trail, it has white blazes.

3. After a short 250m, you enter the Albion Hills Conservation Area. There is a sign asking you to pay at the entrance, which is on Highway 50. I encourage you to pay to help offset the cost of maintaining this wonderful recreational area.

4. Less than 400m later you come to a trail intersection with a kiosk and trail map. Turn left here following the white blazes of the Humber Valley Heritage Trail.

5. Continue following white blazes for over 2k. Look for a sugar shack on the left. You are also on the Albion Hills red trail. You cross a bridge and come to Sign 14. At this point, the white blazes are interrupted for a while. Turn left at Sign 14, taking a double-track trail that is the less worn of the two options. Pass to the right of a single white blaze on a tree, following the trail that climbs gently up to an open farm field.

6. At the top of the ridge at the farm field, turn right following a grassy trail alongside the field. Across the field look for a windmill. It's actually located on a sheep farm you pass later. Up ahead are some lovely elms that as of 2014 had escaped Dutch Elm disease – the epidemic that wiped out most of these beauties.

7. Just past the elm trees, the white blazes reappear. Beside the first white blaze you come to (on your right), there are two bluebird boxes. While these ones are not being maintained, there is a successful program to increase the population of these showy members of the thrush family. The trail swings to the left and heads toward a service road.

8. When you come to the service road, which is actually the entrance to the Albion Hills Community Farm (buy your produce there on Thursday afternoons), turn left and follow the road toward the entrance.

9. Pass by the white blazes of the Humber Valley Heritage Trail that indicate you should turn right before passing through the gates onto Humber Station Road. The Humber Valley Heritage Trail cuts off a bit of road, but can be very wet. Instead, walk out to Humber Station Road.

10. Turn right on to Humber Station Road.

11. After walking about 250m, turn left on to the Caledon Trailway.

12. Follow the Caledon Trailway passing by a sheep farm with a beautiful old hip-roof barn and the windmill. This old railway line passes through some rolling farm fields that are a nice change from the forest.

13. After about 1k you come to a bridge over Mill Lane. Walk across the bridge and take a small path on your right that leads down to Mill Lane below.

14. Turn right on Mill Lane, passing under the bridge that is now overhead. Mill Lane is a hidden oasis in a mostly paved-road environment. You cross a lovely old bridge that spans the Humber River. Given the road's name, there was likely once a mill here.

15. When you come to Humber Station Road, turn right and follow it. It's a not as pretty as Mill Lane, but it's quiet.

16. About 350m down Humber Station Road, you come to Barclay Drive. Turn left on to Barclay Drive and follow it through a rural subdivision. There are a number of these rural subdivisions in Caledon, but they have been largely outlawed in the municipality since they have been deemed a poor use of land. The Town of Caledon now prefers higher density developments. The thought of cutting all that grass exhausts me. Personally, I'd rather be out hiking.

17. Barclay Drive ends at Old Church Road. Turn left on to Old Church Road, but just before you do, notice the lovely, eight-sided house on the northeast corner of this intersection. This is the old Grogan place. I played softball with one of the Grogans. She was a good pitcher with a mean windmill delivery. The current owners do a wonderful job of keeping up this unusual relic.

18. Follow Old Church Road for just over 1k to where you parked on Duffy's Lane. I apologize that you will be walking on a busy road for this last kilometre. To me, it's worth it to get the other 7k of trails or interesting country roads. I hope you agree.

Forks Park /
Brimstone Loop

Pay especially close attention to the directions for this route. There are a number of intersecting trails in the Forks of the Credit Park that can confuse things.

OVERVIEW

This is among Caledon's top five hikes. You walk up Puckering Lane, one of Caledon's hidden roads, and into the Forks of the Credit Provincial Park. You cross the hummocky terrain of the Oak Ridges Moraine where an ocean of milkweed attracts monarch butterflies; bobolinks bop and Baltimore Orioles swoop by in the warm, sunny meadows. I love walking here in the spring when I crave sunshine.

You drop into the Credit River valley and view the ruins of the Cataract Electric Co., before arriving in Caledon's loveliest valley, where I suggest you sit by the roaring Credit River for a picnic. Next it's the hamlet of Brimstone, so named because this was where the tough, though skilled, quarry workers once lived – and fought. Just before little Dominion Street meets the Forks of the Credit Road, you cross a bridge. Look upstream to see the confluence of the west and main branches of the river, which accounts for the name of this area that once echoed with the booming explosions of limestone quarries.

15

Nicola's
Insider Info

LENGTH
12.8 kilometres

LEVEL OF DIFFICULTY
Moderate

LENGTH OF TIME
3 to 4.5 hours

NUMBER OF STEPS
16,951

kCAL BURNED 566

HIGHLIGHTS
Oak Ridges Moraine, Niagara Escarpment, milkweed, kettle lake, Brimstone, wild flowers, wild ginger, Cataract Electric Co. Ltd., Forks of the Credit Park

PLACES TO EAT/DRINK
Take a picnic

ENTRANCE FEE
n/a

GPS

TRAIL MARKER
Loop 15

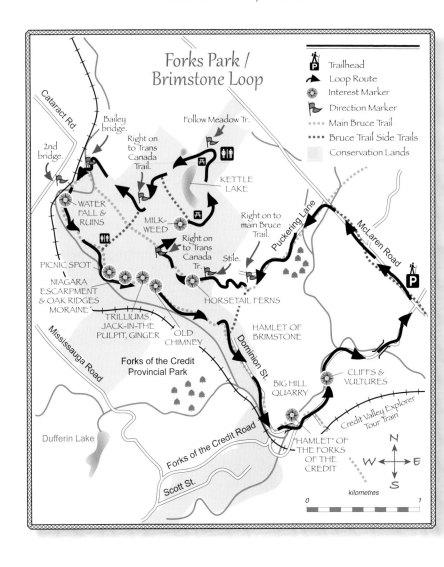

Forks Park / Brimstone Loop

Legend:
- Trailhead
- Loop Route
- Interest Marker
- Direction Marker
- Main Bruce Trail
- Bruce Trail Side Trails
- Conservation Lands

Cataract Rd.

2nd bridge.

Bailey bridge.

Follow Meadow Tr.

Right on to Trans Canada Trail.

KETTLE LAKE

WATER FALL & RUINS

MILK-WEED

Right on to main Bruce Trail.

Right on to Trans Canada Tr.

Stile.

Puckering Lane

McLaren Road

PICNIC SPOT

NIAGARA ESCARPMENT & OAK RIDGES MORAINE

TRILLIUMS, JACK-IN-THE-PULPIT, GINGER

OLD CHIMNEY

HORSETAIL FERNS

HAMLET OF BRIMSTONE

Mississauga Road

Forks of the Credit Provincial Park

Dominion St.

BIG HILL QUARRY

CLIFFS & VULTURES

Dufferin Lake

Forks of the Credit Road

HAMLET OF THE FORKS OF THE CREDIT

Credit Valley Explorer Tour Train

Scott St.

N
W E
S

kilometres
0   1

"To find new things, take the path you took yesterday."

JOHN BURROUGHS

Directions

1. Park on McLaren Road on the north side of the Forks of the Credit Road.

2. Head north (away from the Forks of the Credit Road) on McLaren Road. This is the McLaren Road Side Trail and is marked with the Bruce Trail's blue blazes.

3. After 1.3k, you arrive at little Puckering Lane. Turn left on to Puckering Lane. You are now on the main Bruce Trail.

4. After 1.2k, Puckering Lane splits. Veer right. The trail turns sharply right shortly after the split. Turn right following the main Bruce Trail's white blazes.

Horsetail ferns.

5. The path follows a wire fence for a bit while climbing. After a few turns, you begin descending until you are traversing just below the lip of a steep valley wall, which is above your right shoulder.

6. About 600m after leaving Puckering Lane, you climb over a stile where there is a sign that says "Park Boundary." You are now entering the Forks of the Credit Provincial Park. You are also walking the border between the Niagara Escarpment and the Oak Ridges Moraine. The latter has sandy soils that provide the right environment for a number of plants including some great tufted grass and horsetail ferns. Horsetail ferns are the solo member of their family and are ancient plants dating back to the dinosaurs. To me they look like miniature bamboo.

7. Climb up a sandy hill where there are lots of horsetail ferns. Continue down the other side, go past an unmarked trail that goes to the right where there is a large sign supported by two posts, and take the next unmarked trail that goes right, which is some 300m from the top of the hill. You leave the Bruce Trail here. There is a square post on the left side that advises hikers coming from the trail you are about to take that they have reached the Bruce Trail.

The trail you want only goes to the right. (It would plunge down a very steep hill if it went left.) Take this connector trail that links to the Trans Canada Trail after about 100m.

8. When you come to the Trans Canada Trail, it goes to both the left and right. Go right.

9. Follow the Trans Canada Trail for 1k until you come to a parking lot and washrooms. As you walk this section, you are definitely on the Oak Ridges Moraine. This "hummocky" landscape is typical of a moraine. I love walking along this path. It's wide open and sunny with lots of birds and butterflies. Hot on a July afternoon, but a wonder in the morning or late afternoon or anytime in the spring and fall. There is a sea of milkweed and the chances of seeing a monarch butterfly are good. The trail is flat, the footing is excellent and there is a fabulous picnic table overlooking the lake to your left.

10. Do NOT go toward the parking lot and washrooms (except to use the washrooms). Instead, leave the Trans Canada Trail and veer left on the Meadow Trail. The Meadow Trail rolls along past a kettle lake where there is an excellent picnic table hidden on the left (lake) side of the trail.

11. Just after you pass a hollowed out tree, you come to a trail intersection. Turn right and follow the Trans Canada Trail (once again) along an old road allowance. It eventually drops down a steepish hill into the river valley. You arrive at the Credit River where there is a Bailey bridge.

12. Cross the river on the Bailey bridge. You are now back on the main Bruce Trail with its white blazes.

13. Stick with the Bruce Trail as it rises up a short incline. At the top, there is a metal bridge to your right that goes over the railway tracks. Do NOT turn right (unless you want to look down on the tracks). Both freight trains and the Credit Valley Explorer Tour train (**www.creditvalleyexplorer.com**) use these tracks. They were once part of the Credit Valley Railway that ran from Streetsville to Orangeville. It's a spectacular train trip that includes a ride over the trestle bridge in the Forks of the Credit.

14. Go straight down the slope to another bridge. This one crosses the river at a spot where the water rushes over what was once a dam that was part of the power plant. Behind the dam there used to be an enormous swimming hole.

15. Continue on the main Bruce Trail past the stairs on your left. (Be glad you don't have to climb them.) Follow the trail with a high fence on your right – with lots of warning signs – until you arrive at a viewing platform where you

Where the Credit River forks. PHOTO BY GORD HANDLEY

get a good view of a waterfall and glimpses of the old Cataract Electric Co. It was built by John Deagle in the late 1800s when there was a lot more water in the Credit River. When I was young, at least three kids I knew were swept over this waterfall, some died. The warning signs are there for a reason.

16. Keep following the main Bruce Trail as it re-enters the woods and climbs a bit as it follows a wide path. It eventually drops down as you near one of Caledon's most beautiful meadows.

17. The main Bruce Trail leaves the wide track and turns right taking you toward the river. If you walk 100m past this turnoff, you come to the largest maple tree that I know of in Caledon. It takes at least three people to reach around it.

18. Continue on the main Bruce Trail down to the river until you come to a fabulous spot to stop for a drink, a picnic or to simply soak your tired feet in the fast-flowing river. This is the spot where as kids we met for the Brimstone Ride on Thanksgiving weekend. We'd ride our horses to this spot where my dad and others had already set up a tall tripod and hung an enormous cauldron of onion soup to heat over a wood fire.

19. Follow the white blazes of the main Bruce Trail as it leaves the river heading back into the forest, following an old road that parallels the river. There is a carpet of trilliums and jack-in-the-pulpit along this section of trail in May. There is also a lot of wild ginger and plenty of poison ivy too.

20. Look for a small trail that goes up a steep hill on your left. At the top is a broken-down chimney, which is visible from the road – all that is left of an old building. Take a look, but return to the main trail.

21. Follow the main Bruce Trail until you leave the Forks of the Credit Park at a closed gate and enter the enchanted hamlet of Brimstone. It was once inhabited by reportedly rowdy quarrymen who gave it its name. The quarry managers lived in Belfountain, commuting each day to the Forks of the Credit.

22. As you leave the hamlet look up at the high ridge on your left. This was the site of the Big Hill Quarry, one of the best in the region. Enormous rocks were transported from this quarry to the railway tracks across the valley by a cable car.

23. Follow the road (Dominion Street) as it skirts the river. Keep a look out on your left side for a spot where there are large concrete blocks. On September 29, 2005, after a torrential downpour, the side of the hill let go. Muddy clay covered the road, stranding the residents of Brimstone until the municipality could clear up the mess.

24. After about a kilometre, you arrive at the Forks of the Credit Road where Dominion Street ends. Just before the Forks of the Credit Road, you cross a bridge over the Credit River. Look upstream from the bridge to see where the main and west branches come together. This accounts for the name Forks of the Credit.

25. Turn left on the Forks of the Credit Road, following the white blazes of the main Bruce Trail.

26. After 250m, the main Bruce Trail turns right on to Chisholm Street. Do NOT follow the Bruce Trail; stay on the Forks of the Credit Road.

27. Follow the lovely, but sometimes busy, Forks of the Credit Road for 1.6k until you return to McLaren Road and your car. Take special care since there are some blind curves. It's safest to walk on the outside of blind curves. Be careful!

Forks Park / Meadow Loop

OVERVIEW

This is a happy, sunny baby loop that is great if you have houseguests who aren't enthusiastic hikers. You can amble along this 2-kilometre route without breaking a sweat or your stride. It has some ups and downs, but they are gentle. There are two great spots to have a picnic or snack, and the views of the rolling moraine and a large kettle lake make this route very pleasant indeed.

You are entirely within the Forks of the Credit Provincial Park on this loop that sweeps around the kettle lake. This means you can see the Oak Ridges Moraine and catch glimpses of the Niagara Escarpment. Toronto's infamous developer, Robert Home Smith, once owned this land. Had Smith had his way, Caledon would have been connected to the Humber River in Toronto's west end via an electrical radial railway. The rise in popularity of the automobile ended Smith's lofty plans.

This route is generously sponsored by
In the Hills *magazine* (**inthehills.ca**)

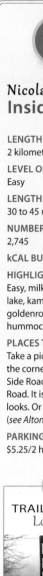

16

Nicola's
Insider Info

LENGTH
2 kilometres

LEVEL OF DIFFICULTY
Easy

LENGTH OF TIME
30 to 45 minutes

NUMBER OF STEPS
2,745

kCAL BURNED 92

HIGHLIGHTS
Easy, milkweed, kettle lake, kames and kettles, goldenrod, sunshine, hummocky terrain

PLACES TO EAT/DRINK
Take a picnic or Café 24 at the corner of Charleston Side Road and Cataract Road. It is better than it looks. Or head into Alton (*see Alton Pinnacle Loop*).

PARKING FEE
$5.25/2 hours or $14/day

GPS

TRAIL MARKER
Loop 16

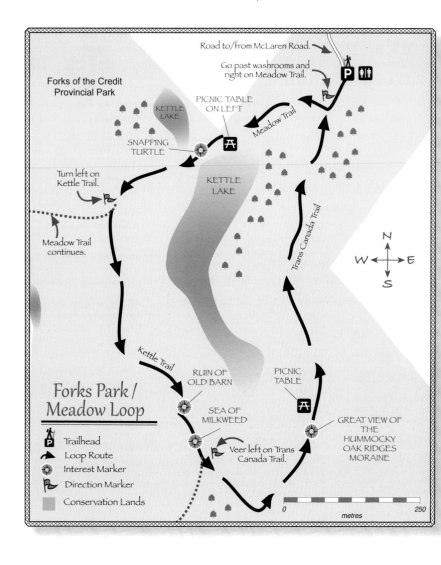

Forks of the Credit
Provincial Park

Road to/from McLaren Road.

Go past washrooms and
right on Meadow Trail.

PICNIC TABLE
ON LEFT

KETTLE
LAKE

SNAPPING
TURTLE

Meadow Trail

KETTLE
LAKE

Turn left on
Kettle Trail.

Meadow Trail
continues.

Trans Canada Trail

N
W — E
S

Kettle Trail

RUIN OF
OLD BARN

PICNIC
TABLE

**Forks Park /
Meadow Loop**

SEA OF
MILKWEED

GREAT VIEW OF
THE
HUMMOCKY
OAK RIDGES
MORAINE

Veer left on Trans
Canada Trail.

🚶 Trailhead
◣ Loop Route
✷ Interest Marker
⚑ Direction Marker
▧ Conservation Lands

0   metres   250

"A pedestrian is a man in danger of his life.
A walker is a man in possession of his soul."

DAVID MCCORD

Directions

Snapping turtle.

1. Park in the Forks of the Credit Provincial Park that you access from McLaren Road, about 2k south of Charleston Side Road. There is a fee to park here ($5.25/2 hours or $14/day), but it gets you very close to the trail, clean washrooms and picnic tables.

2. Follow the trail leaving the parking lot to the right of the washrooms, and turn right on to the Meadow Trail, which is marked with a sign.

3. Follow the Meadow Trail down past the kettle lake where there is a picnic table in a nice sunny spot on the left side of the trail. Pass the lake and go up a slope. I came across a big snapping turtle along here.

4. At the top of the hill, take the Kettle Trail that branches to your left.

5. Follow the Kettle Trail for 500m past the remains of an old barn, proof there was once farming in these hills. Given the Forks of Credit Park is bordered by some of Canada's largest gravel pits, it's likely the farming wasn't as good at the views. The rich aggregate deposits in this area are the result of gravel being backed up by glaciers against the Niagara Escarpment. From high spots, look west. You will see the Niagara Escarpment rise in the distance because the Oak Ridges Moraine meets the Niagara Escarpment in this park.

6. When you come to a sign for the Trans Canada Trail, veer left on it, following it all the way back on the other side of the kettle lake to the Parking Lot. Along the way, you will see the typical hummocky landscape of a moraine. There is also a second picnic table and an ocean of milkweed and goldenrod that in the late summer is sprinkled with purple asters.

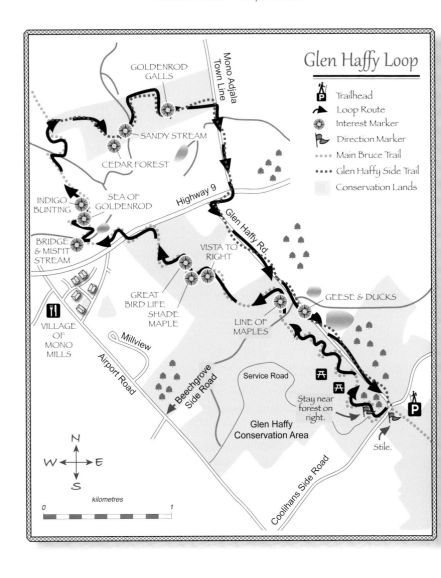

Glen Haffy Loop

- 🚶 Trailhead
- Loop Route
- ✹ Interest Marker
- 🚩 Direction Marker
- •••• Main Bruce Trail
- ▪▪▪▪ Glen Haffy Side Trail
- ▨ Conservation Lands

GOLDENROD GALLS

Mono Adjala Town Line

SANDY STREAM

CEDAR FOREST

INDIGO BUNTING

SEA OF GOLDENROD

Highway 9

Glen Haffy Rd.

BRIDGE & MISFIT STREAM

VISTA TO RIGHT

GEESE & DUCKS

VILLAGE OF MONO MILLS

Airport Road

Millview

GREAT BIRD LIFE SHADE MAPLE

LINE OF MAPLES

Beechgrove Side Road

Service Road

Stay near forest on right.

Glen Haffy Conservation Area

Stile.

N
W   E
S

kilometres
0   1

Coolihans Side Road

"Walking is a man's best medicine."

HIPPOCRATES

Glen Haffy Loop

OVERVIEW

This loop doesn't have any particular view or objective. It's the journey rather than the destination that's important. You pass through forests ranging from deep dark cedar bush where Little Red Riding Hood must have met the wolf, to lovely open maple woods to reforested areas. There are meadows and streams and vistas as well as fabulous bird life. I saw an indigo bunting, which is always a treat, magnificent maples, basswood, elms, yellow birch, locust, white birch, larch, red, white and Scotch pines, hemlock and more. I also saw lots of Monarch butterflies enjoying milkweed, and huge fields of goldenrod. In the forest, there were the remains of trilliums and jack-in-the-pulpit. You even pass a farm where they raise ducks and geese, some of them curiously exotic.

There is a tonne to see on this trail as it goes over hill and dale, much of it through the Glen Haffy Conservation Area, which is owned by Toronto and Region Conservation Authority, and named after the Haffy family who once owned this piece of land. A "glen" is a long narrow valley. Hence, Glen Haffy.

Nicola's
Insider Info

LENGTH
10.7 kilometres

LEVEL OF DIFFICULTY
Moderate

LENGTH OF TIME
2.5 to 3.5 hours

NUMBER OF STEPS
14,829

kCAL BURNED 481

HIGHLIGHTS
Variety, birds, butterflies, exotic ducks and geese

PLACES TO EAT/DRINK
There are no restaurants en route. Market Hill Café in Mono Mills

ENTRANCE FEE
n/a

TRAIL MARKER
Loop 17

Directions

1. Park at the intersection of Coolihans Side Road and Glen Haffy Road just southeast of the village of Mono Mills. There is a wide shoulder with space for several vehicles.

2. Walk west on Coolihans Side Road for 150m until you come to the Bruce Trail sign. Both the white blazes of the main Bruce Trail and the blue blazes for the Glen Haffy Side Trail direct you north into the forest. Climb the stile and follow the white blazes of the main Bruce Trail.

3. When you come to an open field, stay to the right of the picnic tables near the forest.

4. Follow the main Bruce Trail for about 3.5k until you arrive at the very busy Highway 9. Along the way, the trail never seems to stop changing. You pass through airy maple forests with the sun filtering through the foliage, wide-open goldenrod-filled meadows, dense dark cedar bush and reforested pines. Birds abound, and if you are here during the summer, you may see some Monarch butterflies since there is plenty of milkweed for them to feed on. You cross several streams as the trail climbs in and out of a couple of valleys.

5. When you come to Highway 9 cross it carefully. The vehicles move deceptively fast.

6. On the north side of Highway 9, you are no longer in the Glen Haffy Conservation Area. There are a number of signs asking you to not venture off the trail. Please comply with this request. By staying on the designated trail, you assist the Bruce Trail Conservancy in getting more private landowners to allow the trail to cross their land.

7. You descend into a valley, pass by a large pond and then climb up the other side. A bridge crosses over a "misfit stream" in this valley. A misfit stream is one that is too small to have created the valley in which it flows.

8. At the top of the hill, you come to a large meadow filled with goldenrod. I saw a brilliant blue indigo bunting here. While goldenrod is often considered a weed in Canada, it is an ornamental in some gardens in the UK. It forms such a dense mat of roots that it can be almost impossible for farm tractors to plough it under.

9. A little more than 2k from Highway 9, you arrive at a trail intersection where the Glen Haffy Side Trail leaves the main Bruce Trail. Follow the blue blazes of the Glen Haffy Side Trail leaving the main Bruce Trail behind.

Barn along the Glen Haffy Loop.

10. Follow this side trail for 2k until it meets the Mono-Adjala Town Line. Along the way, you pass through a dank cedar forest and some bright reforested areas.

11. Turn right and follow the Mono-Adjala Town Line. You are still on the Glen Haffy Side Trail with its blue blazes. The road passes by several lovely homes. Look for the elegant older white farmhouse on your right.

12. Some 700m later you come to Highway 9 and have to cross it. Once again, be really careful. Turn right once you've crossed Highway 9 and follow it for 150 admittedly painful metres then turn left on to Glen Haffy Road.

13. There are a few farms on this small road. The last one is home to a multitude of geese and ducks. Some of the exotic ones are a sight. After this, it's clear sailing back to your car along another hidden gem of a road that is canopied by tall maples.

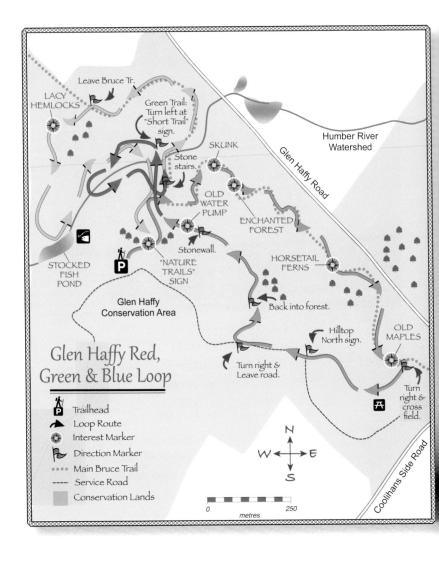

Leave Bruce Tr.

LACY HEMLOCKS

Green Trail: Turn left at "Short Trail" sign.

SKUNK

Stone stairs.

Humber River Watershed

Glen Haffy Road

OLD WATER PUMP

ENCHANTED FOREST

Stonewall.

HORSETAIL FERNS

STOCKED FISH POND

P

"NATURE TRAILS" SIGN

Glen Haffy Conservation Area

Back into forest.

OLD MAPLES

Hilltop North sign.

Turn right & Leave road.

Turn right & cross field.

Glen Haffy Red, Green & Blue Loop

🏳 Trailhead

⚓ Loop Route

⚙ Interest Marker

🚩 Direction Marker

•••• Main Bruce Trail

----- Service Road

⬛ Conservation Lands

N
W E
S

0   250
metres

Coolihans Side Road

"All truly great thoughts are conceived by walking."

FRIEDRICH NIETZSCHE

Glen Haffy Red, Green & Blue Loop

*Glen Haffy Conservation Area
is open from late April until mid-October.*

OVERVIEW

People who prefer hikes without any road-walking will like this route. It is all within the Glen Haffy Conservation Area, named after the Haffy family who once farmed here. A "glen" is a small, secluded valley. Over about two enjoyable hours, you meander through the forest and across open fields. There are picnic tables en route, drinking water and washrooms. You even come upon fishermen trying their talents in a small pond stocked daily with rainbow trout. You pay $5.75 to fish (in addition to your entrance fee) and can take home up to three fish.

This loop route is made up of three separate loop trails so it's a triple loop inside a loop, which makes it a loop de loop de loop de loop, I suppose. First is the red trail, then the green, then the blue. If you have had enough after the red trail (or your kids have), you can bail before the green loop, though I recommend you keep going.

The trails in the Glen Haffy Conservation Area are well marked but only in one direction.

**Nicola's
Insider Info**

LENGTH
5.8 kilometres

LEVEL OF DIFFICULTY
Moderate

LENGTH OF TIME
1.5 to 2 hours

NUMBER OF STEPS
8,466

kCAL BURNED 283

HIGHLIGHTS
No roads, bailout point, stone steps, great trees, Prayer of the Woods

PLACES TO EAT/DRINK
Market Hill Café and other restaurants in Mono Mills

ENTRANCE FEE
Adults $6.50/Seniors $5.50/<14 Free

GPS

TRAIL MARKER
Loop 18

Directions

1. Enter the Glen Haffy Conservation Area through the main entrance on the east side of Airport Road, south of Highway 9. After paying your entrance fee, head to the Lookout Point Parking Area. Pick up a trail map if you can.

2. Park in the Lookout Point Parking area and pass under the Nature Trails sign. Look for the Prayer of the Woods.

3. Follow the red arrows for the Red Trail. It branches to the right heading down into a pretty forest. I came across a skunk (*Mephitis mephitis* or striped skunk) with a feathery plume-like tail rooting in the dirt. It paid absolutely no attention to me so it was fun to observe the little guy. Skunks have poor vision, which accounts for why there are often "dead skunks in the middle of the road, stinkin' to high heaven," and are of course best known for their spray. Its foul smell comes from sulphur-containing chemicals that are sufficiently offensive that bears avoid these otherwise beautiful critters. Humans can smell them from over a kilometre away, and skunks can spray accurately for up to 3m.

4. The route is mostly forested and a lot of it is on the main Bruce Trail, so there are white blazes as well as red arrows. Full of graceful maples and elegant hemlocks, the forest feels enchanted.

5. About half way along the Red Trail, you leave the forest and come to a picnic area in an open field. It's a great place to stop for a break and a nice change from the woods.

6. Continue following the Red Trail as it runs along the edge of the forest you just left. Look for a red arrow on a post. After walking in the open for a while, including along a short section of dirt road, the trail turns right and heads back into the trees. You walk high above some deep gullies, and then leave the forest where a stonewall begins on your right. Stay with the stonewall and the edge of the forest until you come to the Nature Trails sign where you began.

7. Follow the trail back under the Nature Trails sign. This time, pick up the green arrows for the short Green Trail. It's less than 1k long.

8. It takes you down stone steps that were built in the 1950s just after the conservation area opened. People who worked on-site built them from stones found on the property. "At that time," according to the Toronto and Region Conservation Authority, "there were 8 full-time staff at the park so they had

Look for the Prayer of the Woods.

time to tackle large projects like this." The stonewall you passed at Lookout Point was built at the same time.

9. Follow the green arrows around this short loop that skirts a creek bed.

10. When you come to a green arrow and sign saying "Short Trail," turn left following the arrow.

11. When you return to the railing that leads to the stone stairs, DON'T climb up. Instead, follow the blue arrows.

12. The Blue Trail also takes you through the forest and I noticed some gorgeous lacy Eastern Hemlocks. The Blue Trail and main Bruce Trail converge. Make sure you stay on the Blue Trail when the Bruce Trail splits off. You come to a pond stocked with trout where you pay $5.75 to fish and can take home three. Turn left at the pond, following along the edge, and then head back into the woods.

13. When you come back to the railing, head up the stairs and follow the trail back to your vehicle.

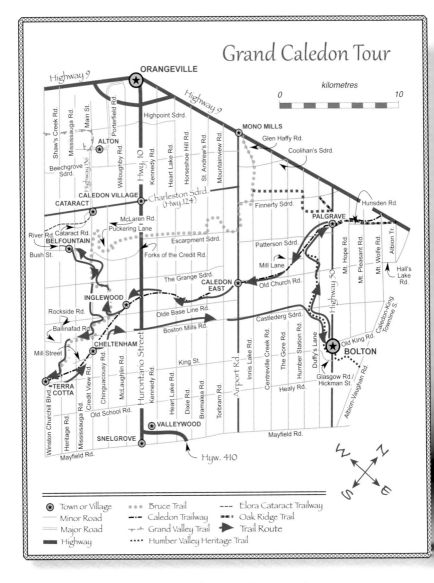

Grand Caledon Tour

"Here at least, on forest trail,
I notice who I am;
The eternal wanderer maybe,
But loving feeling man."

ALEX STRACHAN

Grand Caledon Tour

OVERVIEW

The research for *Caledon Hikes* involved a lot of walking. For months, I spent part of each day with my hiking shoes laced tightly and my GPS in hand. So what better way to celebrate completing all of those loops than by going for a four-day walkabout? In early October, I set off on foot from Belfountain. Four days and over 100k later, I returned home. It was my Grand Caledon Tour. En route I visited Terra Cotta, Cheltenham, Boston Mills, Claude, Bolton, Palgrave, Caledon East and Inglewood. I stayed overnight in Cheltenham, Bolton and Caledon East, and in the latter, I slept in a beautifully restored octagonal house. Different friends accompanied me on various legs of this most pleasant trip.

I had hoped to extend the tour to Alton, but sadly the old Alton Side Trail that followed the McLaren Road allowance north of Charleston Side Road, and linked the Bruce Trail to the Grand Valley Trail is closed, thereby isolating Alton from the trail system. In retrospect, I see that a slightly different route could have included Mono Mills.

Directions

I have only provided a general description of this multi-day route. If you would like a detailed description, contact me at nicolaross.ca. Furthermore, if you would like to help turn this grand tour into a sign-posted route, please let me know. I think it would be a great initiative and am looking for people interested in assisting with the project. I started in Belfountain, but you could also start in Cheltenham, Bolton or Caledon East.

DAY ONE

1. Leave Belfountain following Mississauga Road south toward the Caledon Mountain Estates.
2. Turn into the Caledon Mountain Estates and pick up the main Bruce Trail following it south.
3. At The Grange Side Road leave the main Bruce Trail, continuing south on Credit View Road.
4. Turn left on to Olde Base Line Road for a visit to the Cheltenham Badlands.
5. Follow the main Bruce Trail south from the Cheltenham Badlands all the way to Terra Cotta. Have lunch in Terra Cotta at the Terra Cotta Inn, but make a reservation. We arrived to find the restaurant full. Fortunately, we had food with us and were able to sit on the lovely grounds of the Terra Cotta Inn and munch on our snacks.
6. After lunch, follow the Caledon Trailway to Cheltenham.

DAY TWO

1. Leave Cheltenham via Station Road. Follow Station Road until it comes to Chinguacousy Road where you turn left.
2. At Boston Mills Road, turn right.
3. Follow Boston Mills Road until it becomes Castlederg Side Road on the east side of Airport Road. The names of many roads change when you cross Airport Road because Airport Road was the old boundary between Caledon and Albion townships.
4. Take Castlederg Side Road until you come to the Humber Valley Heritage Trail between Humber Station Road and Duffy's Lane.

5. Follow the Humber Valley Heritage Trail south into Bolton. (There was construction for a new arterial road along this section of the Humber Valley Heritage Trail and it was temporarily closed in 2014.)

6. We stopped at Glen Echo Nursery on Airport Road, where they provided us with coffee, and friends who live on Castlederg Side Road had us for a memorable lunch. You could detour north along Airport Road for a 2.5k round trip and have lunch in Mono Road. There are two restaurants there.

DAY THREE

1. Leave Bolton following the Humber Valley Heritage Trail toward Palgrave. You can pick up the trail in a number of places including across from Edelweiss Park on Glasgow Road or on the west side of Highway 50 across from Colombia Way.

2. Follow the Humber Valley Heritage Trail to Palgrave.

3. Have lunch in Palgrave.

4. After lunch follow the Caledon Trailway west to Caledon East.

DAY FOUR

1. Head west on the Caledon Trailway to Inglewood.

2. Have lunch in the Inglewood General Store.

3. After lunch follow the Caledon Trailway until it crosses Olde Base Line Road.

4. Turn right on to Olde Base Line Road and follow it to Chinguacousy Road where you will pick up the main Bruce Trail.

5. Follow the main Bruce Trail heading north on to Chinguacousy Road. Continue following the main Bruce Trail until you come to the intersection of the Forks of the Credit Road and Dominion Street where the Credit River forks (or un-forks really).

6. Leave the main Bruce Trail here, picking up the Trimble Side Trail as it continues heading west on the Forks of the Credit Road.

7. Follow the Trimble Side Trail until it ends in the Belfountain Conservation Area.

8. Leave the Belfountain Conservation Area, turning left on to the Forks of the Credit Road. Go up the hill out of the valley and cap off your tour with a latte at Higher Ground Coffee Co. in the village.

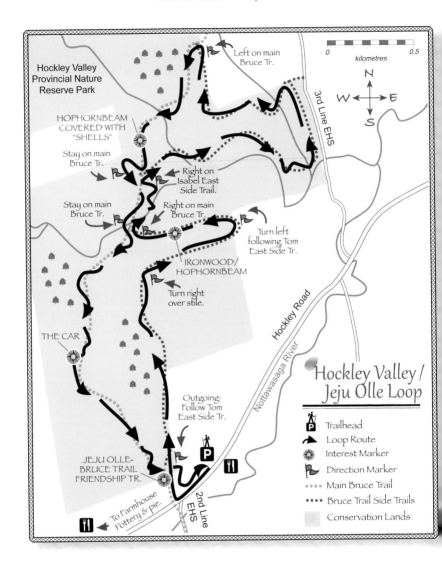

Hockley Valley Provincial Nature Reserve Park

HOPHORNBEAM COVERED WITH "SHELLS"

Stay on main Bruce Tr.

Stay on main Bruce Tr.

THE CAR

JEJU OLLE-BRUCE TRAIL FRIENDSHIP TR.

Left on main Bruce Tr.

Right on Isabel East Side Trail.

Right on main Bruce Tr.

Turn left following Tom East Side Tr.

IRONWOOD/ HOPHORNBEAM

Turn right over stile.

Outgoing: Follow Tom East Side Tr.

3rd Line EHS

Hockley Road

Nottawasaga River

2nd Line EHS

To Farmhouse Pottery & pie.

Hockley Valley / Jeju Olle Loop

- Trailhead
- Loop Route
- Interest Marker
- Direction Marker
- Main Bruce Trail
- Bruce Trail Side Trails
- Conservation Lands

0   kilometres   0.5

N W E S

P

*"We live in a fast-paced society.
Walking slows us down."*

ROBERT SWEETGALL

Hockley Valley / Jeju Olle Loop

OVERVIEW

As I drove down from The Lodge at Pine Cove on the French River on a glorious October day, I stopped for a short hike in the Hockley Valley. It was so beautiful I've included two versions of it even though it's not in Caledon. This longer one is known as the Jeju Olle-Bruce Trail Friendship Trail. It comprises the main Bruce Trail as well as the Tom East Side Trail and the Isabel East Side Trail.

Passing through bright hardwood forests and spooky cedar ones, it crisscrosses braided streams and opens into farmland. Moreover, except for the short walk along the Hockley Road to the trailhead, it is entirely off road. But it is hilly. The Nottawasaga River, which flows through the Hockley Valley, is a "misfit" river in a "re-emergent" valley. A misfit river borrows a valley created in the past by a larger river. During the last ice age, ice blocked the Hockley Valley, stopping the original river's flow. When the ice melted, the valley "re-emerged" with the Nottawasaga, a misfit river.

Look for the sign describing this friendship initiative. The blue, pony-shaped figure known as Ganse is the symbol of the Jeju Olle Trail in Korea. See **www.jejuolle.org**.

*This route is generously sponsored by **The Farmhouse Pottery** on Hockley Road (**pacepottery.com**).*

20

Nicola's Insider Info

LENGTH
11.6 kilometres

LEVEL OF DIFFICULTY
Challenging

LENGTH OF TIME
3 to 4 hours

NUMBER OF STEPS
17,273

kCAL BURNED 559

HIGHLIGHTS
Nottawasaga tributaries, spawning stream, 1939 Chevy, Jeju Olle-Bruce Trail Friendship Trail

PLACES TO EAT/DRINK
Pie at The Farmhouse Pottery, Black Birch Restaurant, Hockley Valley Resort

ENTRANCE FEE
n/a

GPS

TRAIL MARKER
Loop 20

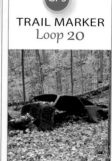

Directions

1. Park in the Bruce Trail lot on the north side of Hockley Road between the 2nd and 3rd lines EHS of the Town of Mono. It is across from the Black Birch Restaurant.

2. Turn right as you leave the parking lot, walking along the north side of Hockley Road – old timers pronounce it Huckley.

3. After 250m, turn right on to the main Bruce Trail with its white blazes. The trail climbs up into a beautiful forest with deep ravines.

4. Less than 200m after leaving the road, you arrive at the Tom East Side Trail. Follow its blue blazes straight ahead. Note the large ash and cedar trees. The emerald ash borer is sadly killing our ash trees so these ones are threatened. Tom East laid out many of the trails in the Caledon section of the Bruce Trail during the 1960s and was president of the Bruce Trail Conservancy. Read about the Jeju Olle Trail and the blue pony. "Jeju Olle is a series of walking routes on Jeju Island, 130km off the southwest coast of Korea. This beautiful UNESCO World Heritage Site is almost sub-tropical in climate, its scenery passing from windswept coastline, through countless tangerine groves crisscrossed by distinctive stone walls, and up to the 6,400-foot [1,950-metre] peak of Mt. Halla."

5. Follow the Tom East Side Trail for 2.5k, sticking to its blue blazes as it wanders down into the forest along some old trail allowances. Look for great vistas of the Hockley Valley to the south. There are some big ironwood trees (aka Hophornbeam).

6. When you come to an intersection with the main Bruce Trail, turn right and head north away from Hockley Road. You climb two stiles and follow white blazes. There are handy maps posted at the major trail intersections.

7. This section of trail goes over a series of bridges spanning a braided stream that feeds into the Nottawasaga River. Keep a close eye for blue blazes so you don't get led down the "garden path," as there are animal trails and unmarked footpaths to lead you astray.

8. Follow the main Bruce Trail as it continues north for just under 1k until you arrive at the Isabel East Side Trail. Turn right here following the blue blazes.

9. About 2k long, the Isabel East Side Trail recognizes Isabel's volunteering activities with the Bruce Trail Conservancy. This pretty section crosses open meadows and dips into dense cedar forest where the trail crosses

the stream again. Look for odd-shaped cedars and the stonewalls of an old barn. Later, a short makeshift trail leads to the creek, which is wide, flat, gravely and has about 10cm of water in it. This is an ideal spawning bed. In the fall, you might observe 30cm-long fish spawning here.

Along the trail.

10. When you come to the Glen Cross Side Trail DO NOT TAKE IT. It goes to a parking lot. Stay left, continuing on the Isabel East Side Trail. Once a town, Glen Cross is now a crossroads.

11. About a 1.4k-climb later, the Isabel East Side Trail meets the main Bruce Trail. Turn left heading back toward Hockley Road following white blazes. Later you meet a "famous" car. (The *Toronto Star* wrote about it.) This 1939 Chevy Master Deluxe sedan was powered by the engine from a 1947 Chevy, according to Mike Vaselenak who tested this section of trail. There isn't anything to salvage now, but this "old gal" earned her keep in the 1950s. Dennis Nevitt and his family used it in their maple sugar operation until it died at this spot in 1956. Note the number of downed trees nearby, likely the result of the December 2013 ice storm.

12. Follow the main Bruce Trail and its white blazes for 3k until you arrive back at sign for the Jeju Olle-Bruce Trail Friendship Trail.

13. Stay on the main Bruce Trail until you come to Hockley Road.

14. Turn left on to Hockley Road until you return to the parking lot.

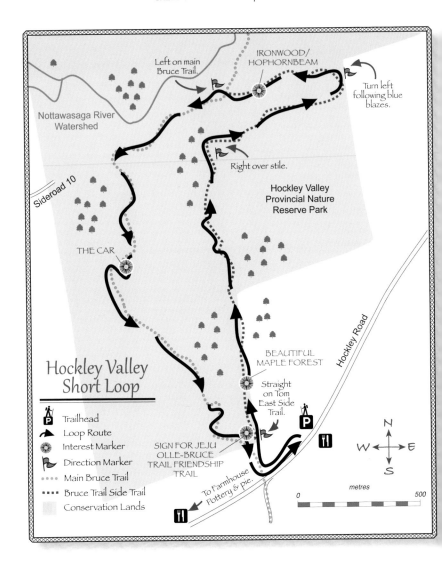

Left on main Bruce Trail.

IRONWOOD/ HOPHORNBEAM

Turn left following blue blazes.

Nottawasaga River Watershed

Right over stile.

Sideroad 10

Hockley Valley Provincial Nature Reserve Park

THE CAR

BEAUTIFUL MAPLE FOREST

Hockley Road

Straight on Tom East Side Trail.

Hockley Valley Short Loop

SIGN FOR JEJU OLLE-BRUCE TRAIL FRIENDSHIP TRAIL

To Farmhouse Pottery & Pie.

Trailhead
Loop Route
Interest Marker
Direction Marker
Main Bruce Trail
Bruce Trail Side Trail
Conservation Lands

N
W E
S

0   metres   500

"Walking is the natural recreation for a man who desires not absolutely to suppress his intellect but to turn it out to play for a season."

LESLIE STEPHEN

Hockley Valley Short Loop

OVERVIEW

This and an earlier hike resulted from a stop I made on a return trip from The Lodge at Pine Cove on the French River. Needing to stretch my legs and wanting to drop in for pie and coffee at The Farmhouse Pottery, I pulled into the Bruce Trail parking lot on Hockley Road. It was one of those clear fall days that make you proud to be Canadian. The trail was carpeted in orange and gold, and as I walked along, leaves floated down around me. I enjoyed the route so much I had to include it in this guide.

Two months later, in December, my partner and I walked the same route after a soggy snowfall on a lead-grey day. Hikers had beaten a path through the snow, and it was wonderful to be outside in the fresh air. But as we chatted away, we twice drifted off the main trail along false starts trampled down by other two- and four-legged walkers.

It was a lesson to me as the author of a hiking guide: Directions that seem straightforward become less so when you are deep in discussion with a friend while hiking along an unfamiliar path.

Directions

1. Park in the Bruce Trail lot on the north side of Hockley Road between the 2nd and 3rd lines EHS of the Town of Mono. It is across from the Black Birch Restaurant.

Nicola's
Insider Info

LENGTH
5.9 kilometres

LEVEL OF DIFFICULTY
Moderate

LENGTH OF TIME
1.5 to 2 hours

NUMBER OF STEPS
8,785

kCAL BURNED 284

HIGHLIGHTS
Fabulous rolling forested trail, 1939 Chevy, Jeju Olle-Bruce Trail Friendship Trail

PLACES TO EAT/DRINK
Pie at The Farmhouse Pottery, Black Birch Restaurant, Hockley Valley Resort

ENTRANCE FEE
n/a

GPS

TRAIL MARKER
Loop 21

2. Turn right as you leave the parking lot, walking along the north side of Hockley Road.

3. After 250m, turn right on to the main Bruce Trail, with its white blazes. The trail climbs up into a beautiful forest with deep ravines.

4. Less than 200m after leaving the road, you arrive at the Tom East Side Trail. Follow its blue blazes straight ahead. Tom East laid out many of the trails in the Caledon section of the Bruce Trail during the 1960s and was president of the Bruce Trail Conservancy. Read about the Jeju Olle-Bruce Trail Friendship Trail at this intersection. This longer route is also included in this guide.

Hophornbeam.

5. Follow the Tom East Side Trail for 2.5k, sticking to its blue blazes as it wanders down into the forest along some old trail allowances. There are great vistas of the Hockley Valley to the south. Look for some big ironwood trees (aka hophornbeam). The lowest branches on hophornbeams are at the perfect height for climbing. Their trunks never get very big around so they look a bit like a miniature tree to me. Their grey bark seems to be peeling.

6. When you come to the main Bruce Trail, turn left following it and its white blazes back toward the Hockley Road.

7. Along the section you meet a "famous" car. (The *Toronto Star* wrote about it.) This 1939 Chevy Master Deluxe sedan was powered by the engine from a 1947 Chevy, according to Mike Vaselenak who tested this section of trail. There isn't anything to salvage now, but this "old gal" earned her keep in the 1950s. Dennis Nevitt and his family used it in their maple sugar operation until it died at this spot in 1956. It's unlikely today's cars have the same staying power.

8. Follow the main Bruce Trail and its white blazes for 3k until you arrive back at sign for the Jeju Olle-Bruce Trail Friendship Trail.

9. Stay on the main Bruce Trail until you come to Hockley Road.

10. Turn left on to Hockley Road and follow it until you return to the parking lot.

Humber River / Duffy's Lane Loop

OVERVIEW

This route is a precious shorter loop that gives you a good bang for your buck. It is less than 5k long and, depending on how often you stop to smell the roses, can be completed in 1.5 hours. It's an easy route to follow through some pretty forests along the banks of the Humber River.

The Humber became a Canadian Heritage River in 1999, but it wasn't without a fight. Sick of it being used as a garbage dump, several women including Florence McDowell, Heather Broadbent and Janet Berton, wife of Pierre, nominated it. When Max Finklestein, who headed up the Canadian Heritage Rivers System program, learned the Humber was seeking a nomination, he reportedly said, "That ditch?" The ladies argued it belonged as it formed part of the Toronto Carrying Place Trail, a historic transportation route that had been used extensively by aboriginal people and Europeans to get from Lake Ontario to Huronia. The ladies finally convinced Finklestein.

There is a higher percentage of road-walking than normal, but Castlederg Side Road is quiet and Duffy's Lane is quieter and very pretty. Walk on the right side as you climb the blind hill on Duffy's Lane.

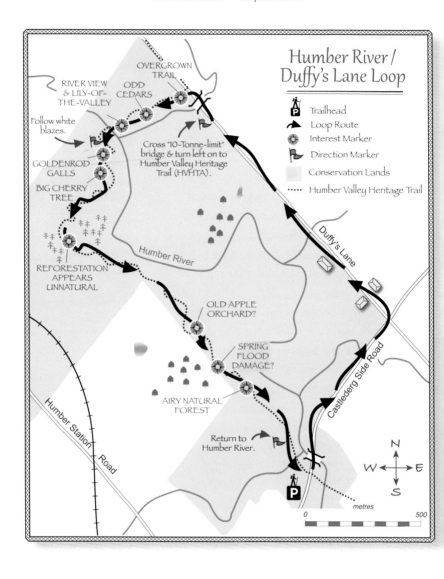

Humber River / Duffy's Lane Loop

Legend:
- Trailhead
- Loop Route
- Interest Marker
- Direction Marker
- Conservation Lands
- Humber Valley Heritage Trail

OVERGROWN TRAIL

RIVER VIEW & LILY-OF-THE-VALLEY

ODD CEDARS

Follow white blazes.

Cross "10-Tonne-limit" bridge & turn left on to Humber Valley Heritage Trail (HVHTA).

GOLDENROD GALLS

BIG CHERRY TREE

Humber River

REFORESTATION APPEARS UNNATURAL

Duffy's Lane

OLD APPLE ORCHARD?

SPRING FLOOD DAMAGE?

AIRY NATURAL FOREST

Castlederg Side Road

Humber Station Road

Return to Humber River.

N W E S

metres
0   500

*"If you are seeking creative ideas, go out walking.
Angels whisper to a man when he goes for a walk."*

RAYMOND INMON

114

Directions

1. Park on Castlederg Side Road between Humber Station Road and Duffy's Lane near the bridge over the Humber River.

2. Head east on Castlederg Side Road for about 750m until you come to Duffy's Lane.

3. Turn left and follow Duffy's Lane for 1.5k. It's a pretty country road with a number of homes to peek at.

4. Cross over a "10-Tonne-Limit" concrete bridge and then look for the Humber Valley Heritage Trail sign (HVHTA) on the left side of the road. This bridge goes over a creek that is actually part of the Humber River. It's hard to believe this is the same river that goes under that large white suspension bridge you can see south of the Gardiner Expressway east of Highway 427 in Toronto.

5. Turn left heading into the ditch past a stile following the white blazes of the Humber Valley Heritage Trail. You follow these blazes for the remainder of this route. It was overgrown along this stretch when I walked it.

6. The trail skirts the Humber River for a bit. There are a couple of boardwalks along this stretch. Look for some oddly shaped cedars.

7. Before the trail climbs slightly leaving the river, look for a patch of lily-of-the-valley on your right. My aunt and uncle once mistook lily-of-the-valley for wild leeks and served them to dinner guests. My uncle managed to call for help before passing out along with everyone else. All survived their serving of *Convallaria majalis*, but it made them very ill. This lovely plant that bears pretty white bell-shaped flowers and red berries contains glycosides that don't agree with your gastrointestinal, circulatory or nervous systems. Look, but don't taste.

8. When you leave the valley, gaze at the field of goldenrod. Look for goldenrod galls: small round balls that are part of the stem. They are home to goldenrod gall flies, which do not harm the plant. They live most of their lives either in the gall or walking on the plant since they don't fly well. Downy woodpeckers peck holes into the galls and eat the insects.

9. You enter a number of reforested areas that are dank compared with natural woods. They are a poor representation of the real thing. While it's great these trees have been planted, artificial forests lack biodiversity and elegance.

Goldenrod galls.

10. The trail drops down a few stairs into a dry streambed (dry in August, that is) that is badly eroded. It looks as if the hard winter of 2013/14 took its toll on this area. Climb a few stairs out of the streambed.

11. Farther down the trail, you walk through a natural deciduous forest that despite being completely canopied feels light and airy. It has a multitude of species growing in the understory.

12. The Humber River reappears on your left and up ahead is a stile that takes you to your car.

Inglewood / Ken Whillans Loop

OVERVIEW

I'd only been in the 88-hectare Ken Whillans Resource Management Area once before I scouted this loop. What a difference 10 years makes. It is now highly accessible; in fact, it's the perfect hike when you are not too sure what to do with visiting family.

The route is absolutely flat and the path is wide enough to walk three or four abreast. Plus, if your 15-year-old daughter says she'll only go on the walk if she can wear her flip-flops, surprise her by saying yes. The footing is that good.

If you or your parents are over 65 or your children are under 18, they can fish without a license and here they might hook warm-water species including bass, pike and sunfish. It's catch and release, and you must use artificial bait and barbless hooks, but there are docks to fish from. Take a picnic. There are lots of tables, some very private.

And who was Ken Whillans? He was the mayor of Brampton from 1982 to 1990 and a former chair of the Credit Valley Conservation board. Whillans drowned while vacationing in Prince Edward Island. He was 63.

> This route is generously sponsored by
> *Caledon Hills Cycling* (**caledonhillscycling.com**).

Nicola's Insider Info

LENGTH
7.2 kilometres

LEVEL OF DIFFICULTY
Easy

LENGTH OF TIME
1.5 to 2.5 hours

NUMBER OF STEPS
9,814

kCAL BURNED 300

HIGHLIGHTS
Great picnicking, fishing, wide, flat, flip-flop-proof trail

PLACES TO EAT/DRINK
Inglewood General Store, Admin office

ENTRANCE FEE
n/a

TRAIL MARKER
Loop 23

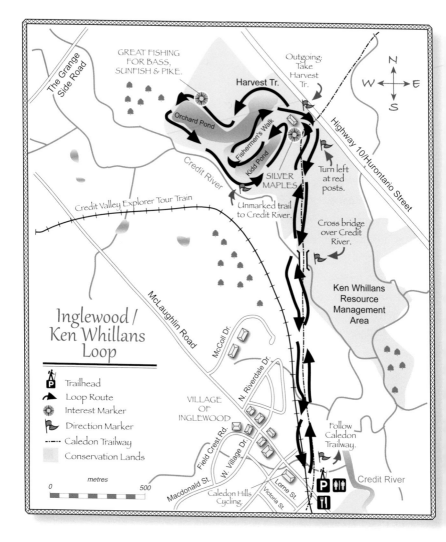

The Grange Side Road

GREAT FISHING FOR BASS, SUNFISH & PIKE.

Harvest Tr.

Outgoing: Take Harvest Tr.

Orchard Pond

Fishermen's Walk

Kidd Pond

SILVER MAPLES

Credit River

Highway 10/Hurontario Street

Turn left at red posts.

Unmarked trail to Credit River.

Credit Valley Explorer Tour Train

Cross bridge over Credit River.

Ken Whillans Resource Management Area

McLaughlin Road

McColl Dr.

Inglewood / Ken Whillans Loop

🅿 Trailhead
➤ Loop Route
✳ Interest Marker
🏴 Direction Marker
-·-·- Caledon Trailway
░ Conservation Lands

metres
0   500

N. Riverdale Dr.

VILLAGE OF INGLEWOOD

Field Crest Rd.

W. Village Dr.

Macdonald St.

Caledon Hills Cycling

Lorne St.

Victoria St.

Follow Caledon Trailway.

Credit River

🅿 🚻 🍴

Directions

1. Park in the village of Inglewood in the lot by the railway tracks. It is on the east side of McLaughlin Road and is designated for users of the Caledon Trailway. (If it's full, you could drive to the Ken Whillans Resource Management Area, which is accessible from Highway 10. There is a larger parking lot there.)

2. Head east on the Caledon Trailway toward Caledon East.

3. The trail is wide and flat. You cross a bridge over the Credit River.

4. After 2k you come to a pair of red metal posts that mark the spot where a trail links to the Ken Whillans Resource Management Area.

5. Turn left here, leaving the Caledon Trailway.

6. On your left there are some magnificent silver maples.

7. After 300m, you arrive at the grey trailer that serves as the Admin Office for the Ken Whillans Resource Management Area. Check in and pay your entrance fees here.

8. Pick up the Harvest Trail. If you walk in a straight line past the Admin Office, you will find the Harvest Trail.

9. This 2.3k-long trail is flat and wide. There are lots of picnic tables and small fishing docks along the way as it skirts Orchard Pond. It is a lovely casual place to walk with a combination of open fields and forest. You will have no idea that you are practically on Highway 10.

10. Continue following this excellent path. After passing Orchard Pond, you come to Kidd Pond. When I saw this name, I realized I was walking in the old Kidd apple orchard. I went to school with Tom Kidd.

11. Look here for a smaller unmarked trail that goes to your right and runs down to the Credit River. It is a short in-and-out if you want the extra distance and would like to wade in the river on a hot afternoon.

12. When you arrive at an interpretive sign about invasive species, a trail called Fisherman's Walk heads to your left. It is only 300m long and is a dead end, but there are some peaceful spots where you can sit on a dock looking out over Orchard Pond or throw in a fishing line.

13. If you took Fisherman's Walk, return to the Harvest Trail and turn left. If not, continue on the Harvest Trail.

14. All too soon you will be back at the Admin Office.

15. The return trip involves retracing your route along the Caledon Trailway to Inglewood where your car awaits. You may want to drop by Caledon Hills Cycling if you are a sporting type. They offer a great selection of athletic gear.

"Everyday I walk myself into a state of well being and walk away from every illness."

SOREN KIERKEGAARD

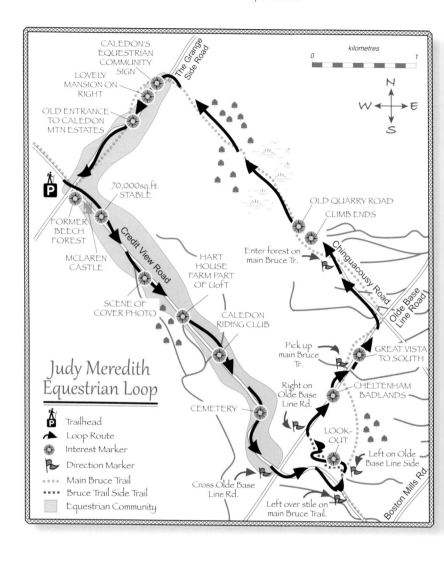

kilometres

0   1

N
W   E
S

CALEDON'S
EQUESTRIAN
COMMUNITY
SIGN

The Grange Side Road

LOVELY
MANSION ON
RIGHT

OLD ENTRANCE
TO CALEDON
MTN ESTATES

P

70,000sq.ft.
STABLE

FORMER
BEECH
FOREST

MCLAREN
CASTLE

Credit View Road

HART
HOUSE
FARM PART
OF UofT

SCENE OF
COVER PHOTO

CALEDON
RIDING CLUB

OLD QUARRY ROAD

CLIMB ENDS

Enter forest on
main Bruce Tr.

Chinguacousy Road

Olde Base Line Road

Pick up
main Bruce
Tr.

GREAT VISTA
TO SOUTH

Right on
Olde Base
Line Rd.

CHELTENHAM
BADLANDS

CEMETERY

LOOK-
OUT

Left on Olde
Base Line Side

Cross Olde Base
Line Rd.

Left over stile on
main Bruce Trail.

Boston Mills Rd.

Judy Meredith
Equestrian Loop

P   Trailhead
   Loop Route
   Interest Marker
   Direction Marker
•••• Main Bruce Trail
•••• Bruce Trail Side Trail
   Equestrian Community

*"I can only meditate when I am walking. When I stop,
I cease to think; my mind works only with my legs."*

JEAN JACQUES ROUSSEAU

Judy Meredith Equestrian Loop

OVERVIEW

This two-hour route has a bit of everything: castles, quarries, horse palaces, cemeteries and, of course, the Cheltenham Badlands. There are hills, but the footing is excellent and you travel long stretches of backcountry roads that allow you and your friends to chat while walking abreast. You delve deep into the countryside on this hike, home to some of Caledon's elite. The trail passes by the McLaren Castle, as well as a 70,000 square-foot horse "palace" and The Caledon Riding Club before entering a dark forest where trees drip with perspiration. If you are lucky you might even see red-jacketed equestrians in hot pursuit of their bushy-tailed quarry as the huntsman's horn echoes in the early morning sunshine.

At about the mid-point, the route leads to Caledon's #1 tourist attraction: the Cheltenham Badlands. The red clay is Queenston Shale. It underlies the entire Niagara Escarpment. These badlands are a Provincially Significant Area of Natural and Scientific Interest, and are unusual in Ontario. Overgrazing likely caused the erosion that may not be good for the environment, but is a delight for visitors.

Take time to admire the crevasses, but resist walking on them as efforts to protect the Cheltenham Badlands are ongoing.

24

Nicola's
Insider Info

LENGTH
10.5 kilometres

LEVEL OF DIFFICULTY
Moderate

LENGTH OF TIME
2.5 to 3.5 hours

NUMBER OF STEPS
14,616

kCAL BURNED 465

HIGHLIGHTS
Equestrian community, quarries, McLaren castle, horse palace, The Caledon Riding Club, Cheltenham Badlands

PLACES TO EAT/DRINK
Nothing en route.

ENTRANCE FEE
n/a

GPS

TRAIL MARKER
Loop 24

Thank you
Have a nice day.

Directions

1. Park on the side of Credit View Road just north of The Grange Side Road.

2. Head south on Credit View Road crossing The Grange Side Road. On the southwest corner of this intersection, there once was a lovely beech forest. Now, the maples have taken over in part because our old beeches have been stricken with Beech Bark Disease. A natural fungus kills the trees after a non-native insect allows it to gain entry. Mature beech trees throughout Caledon are disappearing as a result.

3. Walk down the gentle grade, then look back at the house on your right that backs on the forest. Walk on until you can make out a short stone tower topped by a brown-shingled, pointed roof. This is what has become of the McLaren Castle. Completed in 1864, the McLaren Castle was built of local stone. Its 18 rooms included 9 bedrooms and made it a very imposing "farm residence." An observation platform, surrounded by a heavy stone parapet, sat atop the castle's 15m-tall tower and contributed to the medieval look that made Alexander McLaren's home truly a castle. McLaren was reeve of Caledon Township for 18 years, warden of Peel County in 1880 and his castle housed The Grange Post Office for 40 years. In 1937, a lumber company purchased it, using the castle as a bunkhouse for the lumberjacks who cut down all the trees. Eventually returned to a proper home, fire destroyed it in 1963. The remaining shell was incorporated into the residence before you. As a young child, I slept in the tower in a feather bed.

4. Walk down the road a bit further and look to your left at a magnificent 70,000-square-foot stable and riding arena. The owner's house can't be seen from the road, but aerial photos prove it is equally impressive. As you might guess, you are walking among Caledon's equestrian elite in what is a designated "Equestrian Community." I'm not sure exactly what Judy Meredith thought about this over-the-top stable and arena, but she probably would have liked the equestrian designation. Mother of Tom, Dick and Harry (and Diana who once asked her parents why they hadn't named her "Ann" given she was born between Dick ann Harry), Judy quietly mentored me when I was young. Most of her help involved riding, but we hiked together more recently. For many years, Judy lived along this stretch of road. She died in 2013.

5. See if you can locate the setting for the cover painting of *Caledon Hikes* along this stretch.

6. You pass Hart House Farm, part of the University of Toronto, and then

Happy Thanksgiving.

The Caledon Riding Club. Regardless of your views on fox hunting, a pack of foxhounds in full cry with the huntsman and a field of red-jacketed equestrians in hot pursuit is a spectacle. In the fall, there are hunt meets on Wednesdays and Saturdays at various locations throughout Caledon and points north. Notice the beautiful dry stone fence on your left before you come to the "MacDonald – Settlers of Caledon – 1820" cemetery. Archibald Leith, who died in 1839, was the first person buried here.

7. You follow Credit View Road for 3.5k from The Grange to Olde Base Line Road. Continue south past Olde Base Line Road for another 700m until you come to a sign for the main Bruce Trail. The sign is on the right side of the road, but the trail goes to the left. Turn left here and climb the stile following the white blazes of the main Bruce Trail.

8. After about 300m you come to a fork. Veer left, following the blue blazes for the Olde Base Line Side Trail. You leave the main Bruce Trail.

9. The trail dips down into a valley and comes back up. After 750m, you climb a stile and arrive on Olde Base Line Rd where the Olde Base Line Side Trail ends.

10. Turn right, walking along Olde Base Line Rd until you come to the magnificent Cheltenham Badlands. Take care. There are lots of cars full of rubber-neckers.

11. The Cheltenham Badlands are protected by the Ontario Government as an Area of Natural and Scientific Interest. The property is owned by Ontario

Heritage Trust on behalf of the Bruce Trail Conservancy. The red clay is Queenston Shale. It underlies the entire Niagara Escarpment but is normally buried and out of view. In this location, over-grazing in the 1950s and 1960s exposed the clay. Cellphones are its biggest threat. Cellphones you say? The practice of taking a photo with a cellphone and posting it on Instagram or Facebook has caused the number of people visiting the badlands to explode. Enjoy this amazing place, but please help preserve it by not walking on it. Be a citizen conservationist.

12. Leave the badlands and turn right continuing on Olde Base Line Road. Again, look out for preoccupied drivers.

13. Follow Olde Base Line Road for the next kilometre. It's a paved and sometimes busy road so bear with this part of the route. After picking up the white blazes of the main Bruce Trail, look ahead and just to your right over a beautiful vista. The landscape drops into the Credit River valley. See if you can make out the tall slender spire on the church in Claude.

14. Stay on Olde Base Line Road following the white blazes until you come to Chinguacousy Road.

15. Turn left on Chinguacousy Road, still following the Bruce Trail's white blazes. It's a very quiet and peaceful road that steadily rises. At the top of a steep-ish hill the road turns left into a private drive. You continue straight ahead following the Bruce Trail's white blazes as the path dips into a dense mixed-wood forest.

16. For the next 400m you climb up the escarpment. It's not steep, but it gets your heart pounding. Soon enough, the narrow trail turns into an old quarry road, becomes wider and levels out. Enjoy this respite as you pass through a dense forest with evidence of old quarrying all around you. Look for dugout ponds and discarded cut stones.

17. After you pass the active Deforest Bros Quarries, where they extract beautiful flagstones, look for a narrower track that leaves the road, veering to the left. It is marked by the main Bruce Trail's white blazes. Climb up this trail and turn left on The Grange Side Road and keep heading uphill.

18. At the top of the hill, you re-enter Caledon's Equestrian Community. Look for the sign on your right. Also on your right is an enormous estate situated on land with one of Caledon's best views. It was built by one of the Eaton's store Eatons, though he no longer lives at this address. After 1.5k you arrive back at Credit View Road and your car.

Long Badlands / Devil's Pulpit Loop

25

Nicola's
Insider Info

LENGTH
18.2 kilometres

LEVEL OF DIFFICULTY
Challenging

LENGTH OF TIME
4.5 to 6+ hours

NUMBER OF STEPS
24,811

kCAL BURNED 796

HIGHLIGHTS
Cheltenham Badlands,
lime kiln, lady's slippers,
view, exercise, McLaren
castle

PLACES TO EAT/DRINK
Take lunch as there are
no restaurants along
this route. Head to
Inglewood, Cheltenham
or Belfountain
afterwards.

ENTRANCE FEE
n/a

OVERVIEW

If you want a challenging hike with lots to look at, then this 18.2k route is for you. It takes in some of Caledon's most iconic landmarks including the Cheltenham Badlands, the Devil's Pulpit and the Ring Lime Kiln. If you are a visitor and only have time for one hike, I suggest this one. It takes most of the day.

You begin walking down a quiet country road through farms owned by Caledon's equestrian set. Then it dips into the forest, coming out at the spectacular Cheltenham Badlands. Soon you are back in the forest for a long stretch broken only by The Grange Side Road at a spot partway down Caledon Mountain. The trail then drops to the Credit River where you follow the scenic Forks of the Credit Road before starting the long ascent of the Niagara Escarpment. Along this section you take a side trail into the Mayan-like lime kiln ruins. Then it's up and up, past rare walking ferns until you arrive at a cliff-top lookout over the Credit River valley. It's the best view in Caledon and this hike is among my top five favourites.

TRAIL MARKER
Loop 25

"If you pick 'em up, O Lord, I'll put 'em down."
PRAYER OF THE TIRED WALKER

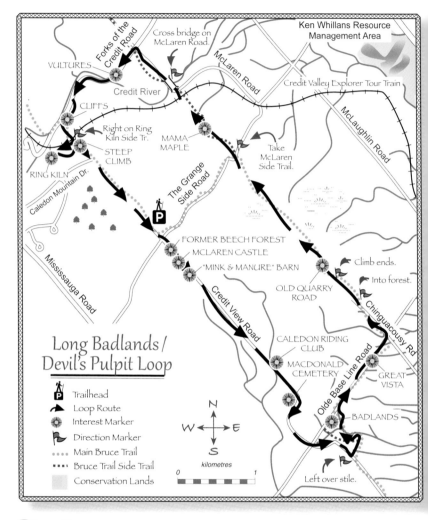

Long Badlands / Devil's Pulpit Loop

Legend:
- Trailhead
- Loop Route
- Interest Marker
- Direction Marker
- Main Bruce Trail
- Bruce Trail Side Trail
- Conservation Lands

Map labels:
Forks of the Credit Road · Cross bridge on McLaren Road. · Ken Whillans Resource Management Area · VULTURES · McLaren Road · Credit River · Credit Valley Explorer Tour Train · McLaughlin Road · CLIFFS · Right on Ring Kiln Side Tr. · MAMA MAPLE · Take McLaren Side Trail. · STEEP CLIMB · RING KILN · Caledon Mountain Dr. · The Grange Side Road · Mississauga Road · FORMER BEECH FOREST · McLAREN CASTLE · "MINK & MANURE" BARN · Climb ends. · Into forest. · OLD QUARRY ROAD · Credit View Road · Chinguacousy Rd · CALEDON RIDING CLUB · MACDONALD CEMETERY · Olde Base Line Road · GREAT VISTA · BADLANDS · Left over stile. · kilometres · N W E S

Directions

1. Park on Credit View Road just north of The Grange Side Road.

2. Head south on Credit View Road crossing The Grange Side Road. On the southwest corner of this intersection, there once was a lovely beech forest, one of the few in this part of Caledon. Now, the maples have taken over, in large part because our old beeches have been stricken with Beech Bark Disease. A natural fungus kills the trees after a non-native insect allows it to gain entry. Mature beech trees throughout Caledon are disappearing.

3. Walk down the gentle grade then look back at the house on your right that backs on the forest. Walk on until you can make out a short stone tower topped by a brown-shingled, pointed roof. This is what has become of the McLaren Castle. Completed in 1864, the McLaren Castle was built of local stone. Its 18 rooms included 9 bedrooms and made it a very imposing "farm residence." An observation platform, surrounded by a heavy stone parapet, sat atop the castle's 15m-tall tower and contributed to the medieval look that made Alexander McLaren's home truly a castle. McLaren was reeve of Caledon Township for 18 years, warden of Peel County in 1880 and his castle housed The Grange Post Office for 40 years. In 1937, a lumber company purchased it, using the castle as a bunkhouse for the lumberjacks who cut down all the trees. Eventually returned to a proper home, fire destroyed it in 1963. The remaining shell was incorporated into the residence before you. As a young child, I slept in the tower in a feather bed.

4. Walk down the road a bit further and look to your left at a magnificent 70,000-square-foot stable and riding arena. The owner's house can't be seen from the road, but aerial photos prove it is equally impressive. You are walking in Caledon's only designated "Equestrian Community."

5. See if you can locate the scene for the cover painting of *Caledon Hikes* along this stretch.

6. You pass Hart House Farm, part of the University of Toronto and then The Caledon Riding Club. The Caledon Pony Club meets here. It is similar to 4H and teaches children the basics of riding as well as how to care for their mounts. It's a great organization, part of an international movement. Farther along, notice the lovely stone house with a fabulous dry stone fence on your left before you come to the "MacDonald – Settlers of Caledon – 1820" cemetery. Archibald Leith, who died in 1839, was the first person buried here.

7. Follow Credit View Road for 3.5k from The Grange Side Road to Olde Base Line Road. Continue south past Olde Base Line Road for another 700m until you come to a sign for the main Bruce Trail that is on the right side of the road. Turn left here, climb the stile and follow the white blazes of the main Bruce Trail.

8. After 300m you come to a fork in the path. Veer left, following the blue blazes for the Olde Base Line Side Trail.

9. The trail dips down into a valley and then comes back up. After 750m, you climb a stile onto Olde Base Line Road where the Olde Base Line Side Trail ends.

10. Walking along Olde Base Line Road until you come to the magnificent Cheltenham Badlands. Take care along this busy stretch of road.

11. The Cheltenham Badlands are protected by the Ontario Government as an Area of Natural and Scientific Interest. The property is owned by Ontario Heritage Trust on behalf of the Bruce Trail Conservancy. The red clay is Queenston Shale. It underlies the entire Niagara Escarpment but is normally buried and out of view. In this location, over-grazing in the 1950s and 1960s exposed the clay. Enjoy this amazing place, but please help preserve it by not walking on it. Be a citizen conservationist.

12. After visiting the badlands, continue east on Olde Base Line Road until you come to Chinguacousy Road. Along the way, you pick up and follow the main Bruce Trail's white blazes. It's a paved road and can be busy so you just have to bear with this part of the route.

13. Turn left on Chinguacousy Road. This is a peaceful gravel road.

14. You climb steadily. At the top of a steepish hill the road turns left into a private drive. You continue straight ahead following the Bruce Trail's white blazes into a dense mixed-wood forest.

15. For the next 400m you climb. It's not steep, but it's steadily up. The narrow trail turns into an old quarry road, becomes wider and levels out.

16. Meander along this old road deep in the forest, past the active Deforest Bros Quarries where they quarry beautiful flagstones.

17. Some 2k from where you arrived at the flat quarry road, follow a narrower track that veers to the left and climbs to The Grange Side Road. It is marked with white blazes.

18. When you arrive at The Grange Side Road, the white blazes of the main Bruce Trail go to the left up the hill.

19. DO NOT follow the main Bruce Trail. Instead, turn right and follow the blue blazes of the McLaren Road Side Trail that begins here by heading down The Grange Side Road.

20. Almost immediately, it turns left and enters the forest on a muddy trail.

21. Follow this trail, which dries out after about 100m. Soon you will see a great vista off to your right. Then the trail drops down into an older growth forest. There is a big mama maple just to the right of the trail.

22. Continue down the forested slope until the trail comes out on to a set of railway tracks. Both freight trains and the Credit Valley Explorer Tour train use these tracks. They were once part of the Credit Valley Railway. It's a

spectacular train trip over the trestle bridge in the Forks of the Credit.

23. The trail continues down a steep slope on the other side of the railway tracks coming out onto McLaren Road at a single-lane concrete bridge. (There is talk of replacing the bridge.)

Members of Caledon's equestrian community.

24. Continue over the bridge under which flows the Credit River. There was once a trout hatchery just past the bridge and you are not far from the grand Caledon Mountain Trout Club. You are still following the blue blazes for the McLaren Road Side Trail.

25. When you come to the Forks of the Credit Road turn left, leaving the McLaren Road Side Trail.

26. Follow the Forks of the Credit Road passing the old ice cream shop and skirting the river. Look up to your left and you will see the Niagara Escarpment's cliffs soaring overhead. Look for big black vultures. They love gliding on the updrafts here. This valley is brilliant in the fall as the red-coloured maples, white birches and evergreens put on a display.

27. After 1.7k you come to Chisholm Street. Turn left here by a cauldron planted with lovely flowers. You are now back on the main Bruce Trail with its white blazes.

28. At the end of little Chisholm Street look for the old brick schoolhouse behind a high fence.

29. The trail enters the forest and starts up a steep incline.

30. After 200m and out of breath, you come out on to the railway tracks. Cross them and re-enter the forest.

31. The climb continues for about 125m where you will see the signs for the Ring Kiln Side Trail.

32. Turn right here following the blue blazes for 600m. It takes you to the remains of a lime kiln though it looks more like something out of an Indiana Jones movie. It's well worth the 600m excursion.

The final "ascent."

33. After exploring the lime kiln and, if you are there in late June, looking for yellow Lady's Slipper orchids, return to the main Bruce Trail following the trail you just came in on.

34. When you reach the main Bruce Trail, turn right following the white blazes up hill.

35. You climb through an amazing rock garden in a dense cedar forest. It feels more like the BC coast than southern Ontario.

36. Keep climbing until you reach the base of a sheer cliff and a set of crude stone stairs. Use the cable to help you make your way to the top of the escarpment.

37. At the "summit," take a break and look out over the view. In the distance you can see an enormous lone house. It sits on the old Eaton estate. Queen Elizabeth stayed there once.

38. In late September and the first half of October, this is the place to be to see the fall colours.

39. When you have caught your breath and had some water, continue on the trail. In the spring, there are great trilliums along this stretch.

40. Soon the trail crosses Caledon Mountain Drive.

41. Stay straight following the white blazes of the main Bruce Trail.

42. This is a lovely piece of rolling trail that travels though a typical upland forest of maple, basswood and ash trees. It turns into a wider track that was once an old road, but is now overgrown.

43. The route follows what is actually the unopened road allowance for Credit View Road. This part of the Bruce Trail was one of the last to open. The trail builders were having trouble finding a route down the escarpment until they recognized the road allowance. Not only was it open to public use, it also descended the escarpment at one of the least steep places.

44. You are buried in the bush along here, far from cars and computers. In time, the trail arrives at a green gate and then a driveway on the right. Up ahead is your parked car.

McLaren Loop

OVERVIEW

This loop leads you into one of Caledon's prettiest valleys. Art Bracken's old farm stretches out before you and it's easy to imagine his big-eyed Jersey cows grazing languidly on rich pasture. There is more time spent walking on roads than normal, but they are small gravel ones, and the longest portion is closed in the winter because of its steep grade. You walk all the way down Caledon Mountain in one fell swoop, then pass under the iconic "graffiti bridge" near the original site of the Caledon Ski Club. But before you do, you get an uncommon glimpse of the very private Caledon Mountain Trout Club.

You also have an energetic and, by Southern Ontario standards, steep climb up the cliffs of the Niagara Escarpment. But you pass through an amazing rock garden where moss and rare walking ferns abound. There is a cable to assist you on the final ascent up some rustic stone steps and when you "summit," it's all worthwhile. Perhaps the best view in Caledon awaits. With vultures soaring at eye level, you look over a sea of forest – green in summer and blazing orange, red and yellow in early October. Lace up your boots.

> *"Walking would teach people the quality that youngsters find so hard to learn — patience."*
>
> EDWARD P. WESTON

26

Nicola's
Insider Info

LENGTH
8.4 kilometres

LEVEL OF DIFFICULTY
Moderate

LENGTH OF TIME
2 to 3 hours

NUMBER OF STEPS
11,311

kCAL BURNED 440

HIGHLIGHTS
Old Caledon Ski Club, Caledon Mountain Trout Club, graffiti bridge, Caledon mountain, Devil's Pulpit, views, walking fern, rock garden, Credit Valley Explorer Tour train

PLACES TO EAT/DRINK
Nothing en route. Inglewood and Belfountain are close by.

ENTRANCE FEE
n/a

GPS

TRAIL MARKER
Loop 26

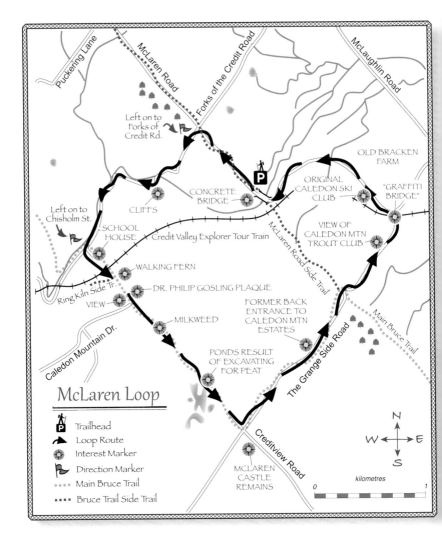

McLaren Loop

- Trailhead
- Loop Route
- Interest Marker
- Direction Marker
- Main Bruce Trail
- Bruce Trail Side Trail

(Map labels:) Puckering Lane · McLaren Road · Forks of the Credit Road · McLaughlin Road · Left on to Forks of Credit Rd. · OLD BRACKEN FARM · CONCRETE BRIDGE · ORIGINAL CALEDON SKI CLUB · "GRAFFITI BRIDGE" · Left on to Chisholm St. · CLIFFS · SCHOOL HOUSE · Credit Valley Explorer Tour Train · VIEW OF CALEDON MTN TROUT CLUB · McLaren Road Side Trail · WALKING FERN · DR. PHILIP GOSLING PLAQUE · Ring Kiln Side Tr. · VIEW · MILKWEED · FORMER BACK ENTRANCE TO CALEDON MTN ESTATES · Caledon Mountain Dr. · PONDS RESULT OF EXCAVATING FOR PEAT · The Grange Side Road · Main Bruce Trail · Creditview Road · McLAREN CASTLE REMAINS · N W E S · kilometres · 0 · 1

Directions

1. Park on McLaren Road, about 1k south of the Forks of the Credit Road near the old concrete bridge. Be sure to avoiding parking in the area with no parking signs. (This bridge is being assessed so may not be an "old concrete bridge" for long. Pity if it has to be replaced.)

2. Head north on McLaren Road toward the Forks of the Credit Road.

3. Turn left on to the Forks of the Credit Road.

4. Follow the Forks of the Credit Road for 1.7k until you come to Chisholm Street. It is small and only runs to the left. While walking along the Forks of the Credit Road, you follow the Credit River – a great trout stream. Also look up at the cliffs of the Niagara Escarpment that form a wall high above you. This road can be busy on weekends, but during the week it is lovely and quiet. Nonetheless, take care and consider walking on the outside of blind corners.

5. Turn left on to Chisholm Street following the white blazes of the Bruce Trail.

Credit River.

6. After you pass an old red brick schoolhouse (behind a high fence) that has been converted into a private home, the trail enters the forest and climbs for 120m to the top of the escarpment.

7. First you climb steep steps to an active railway that carries both freight trains and the Credit Valley Explorer Tour train, which runs from Orangeville to Streetsville and back along tracks build by the Credit Valley Railway. Look for trains before crossing the tracks.

8. Keep climbing on the other side of the tracks, following the white blazes of the Bruce Trail.

9. You come to the Ring Kiln Side Trail. If you want to explore, this is a 1.2-k side trail that goes to an amazing spot. The old lime kiln looks like a Mayan ruin. This area of Caledon was heavily quarried in the late 1800s. The lime kiln, slag piles of rocks and a pair of steel rails are all that remain.

10. Farther up the trail, you walk through an amazing rock garden. The footing can be slippery so take care. The limestone is moss covered and snow can lurk in the deep crevasses as late as July. Keep an eye out for the rare walking fern. (*See photo on page 79.*)

11. Finally, you come to the cliff. A wire cable helps you negotiate stone steps to the "summit." In all, you will climb up 120m over 0.5k.

12. At the top, take a break and look out from the viewpoint over perhaps the best view in Caledon.

13. Carry on along a mercifully flat trail, past the commemorative plaque to Dr. Philip Gosling, one of the Bruce Trail founders and a recipient of the Order of Canada, who also contributed to the Foreword of this book.

14. If you are hiking in May, look for glorious white trilliums along this stretch of the trail.

15. At the paved Caledon Mountain Drive, continue straight ahead following the white blazes of the Bruce Trail.

16. You enter the forest again, climbing a bit before the trail settles down and eventually merges with an old dirt track at a T-intersection where you veer left. Follow the track (and the Bruce Trail's white blazes) until you come to a gate and the start of Credit View Road.

17. Follow Credit View Road for about 150m to The Grange Side Road. (From the top of the cliff – Gosling Plaque – to The Grange Side Road is about 1.5k.)

18. Turn left onto The Grange Side Road, following the Bruce Trail's white blazes.

19. Follow this quiet gravel road for a little over 2k until you come to the top of a steep hill where there are gates that close the road in winter. Partway down the hill, the main Bruce Trail turns right, then the McLaren Road Side Trail goes left. DO NOT FOLLOW THEM. STAY ON THE ROAD. As you drop down, there are sweeping views of the valley below. Near the bottom, you can make out the Caledon Mountain Trout Club, a large white building buried in trees to the north. This is the only place that I know of where you can catch a glimpse of this historic clubhouse. It has been operating as the Caledon Mountain Trout Club since 1901. Costing $22,000, the clubhouse opened two years later. From the top of the hill until you arrive at the "graffiti bridge" as it's known locally, you drop back down 120m, but over twice the distance (about 1k). Just before passing under this trestle bridge (at 2220 The Grange Side Road) is the entrance to the original location of the Caledon Ski Club. A tractor powered the sole rope tow and the clubhouse was a converted chicken coop. After several successful seasons here, the club moved to its current location on Mississauga Road in 1962.

20. Turn left on to McLaren Road immediately after the graffiti bridge and follow it for 1.6k to where you parked your car.

Moraine Meets Escarpment Loop

The trails in the Forks of the Credit Park are well marked, but there are intersecting trails, so pay particularly close attention to these directions.

OVERVIEW

This 2-hour loop gives you an inside-out look at Caledon. Taking place entirely within the Forks of the Credit Provincial Park, it offers vistas of wide-open hummocky terrain typical of a moraine, and stretches of the Credit River as it cascades down the escarpment in the lee of high cliffs. It is here that two of Ontario's major landforms – the Oak Ridges Moraine and the Niagara Escarpment – collide.

The route passes the ruins of the old Cataract Electric Co. that powered nearby communities before flooding stripped owner John Deagle of his ambitious plans. With flow that is a fraction of what it was in the early 1900s, it's still a big waterfall and several of my schoolmates succumbed to its might.

The trail takes you past what is perhaps Caledon's largest maple tree and into the most beautiful valley, where you can stop by the river for a picnic.

The path then sweeps up through a maple forest that is blanketed in spring with trilliums, jack-in-the-pulpit, wild ginger and bloodroot, before passing the remains of an old farmstead and skirting a kettle lake. It's hard to imagine settlers had much success tilling the gravel that lies below.

Nicola's Insider Info

LENGTH
6.8 kilometres

LEVEL OF DIFFICULTY
Moderate

LENGTH OF TIME
1.5 to 2.5 hours

NUMBER OF STEPS
9,498

kCAL BURNED 307

HIGHLIGHTS
Kettle lake, kames and kettles, Cataract Electric Co., sunny hummocky terrain, beautiful valley, goldenrod, milkweed, wildflowers, large maple

PLACES TO EAT/DRINK
Take a picnic or see Alton Pinnacle Loop

ENTRANCE FEE
$5.25/2 hours, $14/day

GPS

TRAIL MARKER
Loop 27

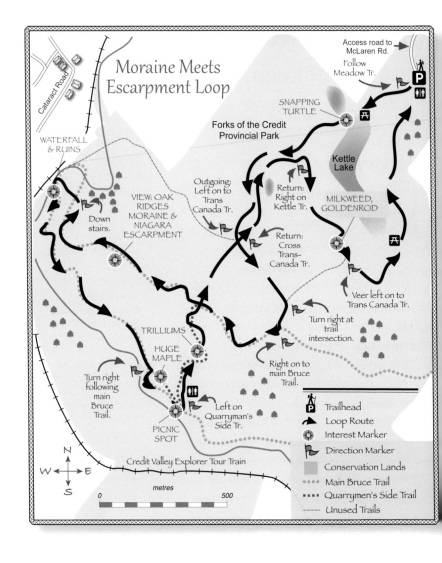

Moraine Meets Escarpment Loop

Cataract Road

WATERFALL & RUINS

Forks of the Credit Provincial Park

SNAPPING TURTLE

Access road to McLaren Rd.
Follow Meadow Tr.

Kettle Lake

MILKWEED, GOLDENROD

VIEW: OAK RIDGES MORAINE & NIAGARA ESCARPMENT

Down stairs.

Outgoing: Left on to Trans Canada Tr.

Return: Right on Kettle Tr.

Return: Cross Trans-Canada Tr.

Veer left on to Trans Canada Tr.

Turn right at trail intersection.

TRILLIUMS

HUGE MAPLE

Turn right following main Bruce Trail.

Left on Quarryman's Side Tr.

PICNIC SPOT

Right on to main Bruce Trail.

Credit Valley Explorer Tour Train

Legend:
- 🅿 Trailhead
- ⬆ Loop Route
- ✴ Interest Marker
- ⚑ Direction Marker
- ▨ Conservation Lands
- ⋯ Main Bruce Trail
- ▪▪▪ Quarrymen's Side Trail
- ‒‒‒ Unused Trails

N W E S

metres
0   500

"I only went out for a walk, and finally concluded to stay out until sundown: for going out, I found, was really going in."

JOHN MUIR

Credit River Explorer Tour train. PHOTO BY GARY HALL

Directions

1. Park in the designated lot for the Forks of the Credit Provincial Park that you access from McLaren Road south of Charleston Side Road. There is a parking fee but you are close to the trail and washrooms.

2. Follow the trail as it leaves the parking lot to the right of the washrooms and turn right on to the Meadow Trail, which is marked with a sign.

3. Follow the Meadow Trail down to the kettle lake where there is a picnic table (in summer) in a sunny spot, and then up a slope past the lake.

4. Continue on the Meadow Trail for about 1k, passing by the Kettle Trail.

5. When you come to a marked intersection with the Trans Canada Trail, turn left on to the Trans Canada Trail, which follows an old road allowance.

6. After 300m, you come to a trail intersection, turn right. The trail narrows. In 100m, you will arrive at a T-junction on the ravine edge where there is a sign advising you are now on the Bruce Trail. Turn right and follow the main Bruce Trail's white blazes along the ravine edge.

7. After 400m you come to The Quarryman's Side Trail. Pass it by, going straight ahead.

8. Follow the trail as it skirts the edge of the Credit River valley. There are some good lookouts. You may even spy a train going by on the other side of the valley. After 1k, you come to another trail intersection. The main Bruce Trail with its white blazes turns right. DO NOT take it. Instead, turn left, heading down the long set of stairs.

9. At the bottom of the stairs, turn left and go to the viewing platform over the waterfall and ruins of the Cataract Electric Co. Built by John Deagle in the late 1800s, it powered many nearby communities. Flooding swamped the plant and it was eventually purchased by Ontario Hydro and decommissioned. Across the valley, spring water is still tapped from a well that was the first used to make Canada Dry Ginger Ale©, the "Champagne of Ginger Ales."

10. Continue on following the white blazes of the Bruce Trail. The trail enters the forest and climbs before dropping into the loveliest valley in Caledon.

11. Almost 1k after leaving the viewing platform, the main Bruce Trail turns right, leaving the old roadway you've been following. (If you continue down the old road for about 100m, there is the largest maple tree I know of in Caledon. It takes at least 3 people to reach around it.)

12. Follow the main Bruce Trail to the Credit River. At the intersection with The Quarryman's Side Trail stop for a picnic on the river's edge.

13. Afterwards, follow the blue blazes of The Quarryman's Side Trail as it heads away from the river, enters the forest and climbs up the ridge. En route, you will pass by some washrooms.

14. In the forest, look for trilliums, jack-in-the-pulpit, wild ginger and bloodroot; they abound here in spring.

15. You will be huffing when you reach the top of this hill where The Quarryman's Side Trail ends. Cross over the main Bruce Trail, continuing straight ahead.

16. A short 250m later, you come to a marked intersection. Continue straight on the Meadow Trail crossing the Trans Canada Trail.

17. After 500m, turn right on the Kettle Trail. It takes you around the other side of the kettle lake on a trail with lovely views of the lake and open meadows. Milkweed abounds here and in the fall, goldenrod mixed with purple asters provide a stunning combination. There are plenty of apple trees for those who like their fruit tart. These fruit trees are a sure sign that cattle once grazed these hills. Another clue is the ruin of an old barn on the left side of this trail.

18. At the next fork in the trail veer left on to the Trans Canada Trail.

19. Less than 1k later and much too soon, you are back at your car.

Oak Ridges Moraine Loop

Be extra diligent on this route as there are intersecting trails, twists and turns. Trail markers can be obscured where the trail is overgrown. It's not easy to follow.

OVERVIEW

My friend Neil Morris cobbled together this brilliant 9.5k loop. Impressively, it connects the Oak Ridges Trail, the Caledon Trailway, the Simcoe County Forest and the Tottenham extension to the Caledon Trailway. That being said, this route is not as well marked as others in this book. So keep your eyes tuned to blazes, map and directions as you walk through fields and forests on this most agreeable hike.

The Oak Ridges Moraine, which extends for 160k from the Niagara Escarpment to the Trent River system, is an interlobate moraine because it was laid down in a trough between two lobes of receding glaciers. Sands, silts and gravel filled this trough until a ridge developed. When the glaciers disappeared, the ridge – the Oak Ridges Moraine – remained. Often too gravelly to farm, moraines provide a great service by purifying water. You will see its characteristic "hummocky" or hilly terrain.

Some of this trail is outside Caledon, but it begins and ends within the Town's borders, so I snuck it in.

"Thoughts come clearly while one walks."

THOMAS MANN

Nicola's
Insider Info

LENGTH
9.5 kilometres

LEVEL OF DIFFICULTY
Moderate

LENGTH OF TIME
2.5 to 3.5 hours

NUMBER OF STEPS
13,043

kCAL BURNED 409

HIGHLIGHTS
Oak Ridges Moraine, great gabbing along the Caledon Trailway, catalogue house

PLACES TO EAT/DRINK
Fresh-cut fries stand, if open

ENTRANCE FEE
n/a

TRAIL MARKER
Loop 28

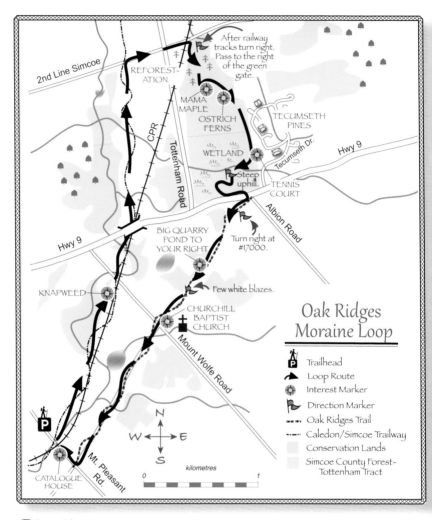

Directions

1. Park in one of the spaces available where the Caledon Trailway crosses Mount Pleasant Road just south of Highway 9.

2. Walk north toward Tottenham on the Caledon Trailway. The soccer and recreation area to your right is a private camp run by Slovenians since the 1950s.

3. Cross Mount Wolfe Road on the Caledon Trailway.

4. Pass under Highway 9 as you enter Simcoe County on a pleasant stretch of rail trail. Rail trails are too flat and straight for my taste, but what they lack

in topography they make up for in allowing you and your friends to walk two or three abreast and gab. If it's late July or early August, notice the big patches of knapweed. It has pretty mauve flowers. Lovely to look at, but it's very invasive and crowds out other native species.

5. After following the rail trail for about 3.5k, you arrive at the 2nd Line of Simcoe. Turn right and walk along this quiet road. (There is no road sign – if you get to the "Wildlife Café" sign, you have gone too far.) It's the first road you come to.

6. Follow the 2nd Line, crossing Tottenham Road with caution.

7. Just after Tottenham Road, walk over a set of railway tracks (used by fast-moving freight trains). Turn right into the Simcoe County Forest (Tottenham Block) just after the railway tracks.

8. Follow the trail toward a green metal gate, keeping to the right of the gate. (The green markers also go to the left, away from the green gate, at this trail junction.) The trail you follow (to the right of the gate) will be occasionally marked with green blazes.

9. Pass the gate (on the right side), then veer left and then left again. You walk through an open reforested area that seems to have been thinned.

10. Go straight across the next trail you come to continuing to follow the green blazes. This is the first climb on this loop.

11. When you come to a T-intersection, turn left, following the green blazes.

12. When you come to the next intersection of trails, look on your left for an old white pine, a real mama tree. This massive tree is pretty much the halfway marker for this loop. Continue straight ahead crossing the other trail. There are several pinky-red and green blazes. Look for some lovely ostrich ferns. They produce fiddleheads in the spring.

13. You arrive at another intersection of trails of sorts. Go straight following the trail with some houses to your left. The pinky-red blazes have abandoned you, but the green blazes are still there. These houses are part of the Tecumseth Pines retirement community. Nice folks, but obey the "Private Property" signs on your left.

14. Keep walking along the fence line with the houses and signs to your left. The trail veers right near a tennis court and two private property signs.

15. The trail passes through a wetland complex that looks as if it could be wet in the spring, so make sure you have appropriate footwear. The trail gets pretty overgrown here, so keep an eye out for the green blazes.

16. At the next intersection of trails, go left. You are still in the wetland area.

17. The trail climbs steeply out of the wetland. At the top of the hill, turn right at the T-intersection, leaving the green blazes. Do not turn left down the hill, even if it seems like the more obvious route.

18. Go left at the next intersection of trails after you go down a small slope, and then left again so that you are now walking parallel to Highway 9, which is not very far away.

19. Follow this parallel route until you come to a green gate at the entrance to the Simcoe County Forest (Tottenham Block).

20. Leave the forest by climbing over the green gate, turn left and walk along Highway 9. The road allowance is very wide, so you can walk along the grassy bank on the north side of Highway 9 well away from vehicles. Look for a "Fresh Cut Fries" stand. If it's open, you might treat yourselves.

21. After a short 150m along Highway 9, walk down the bank and carefully cross the highway. It is VERY busy, so be careful.

22. On the other side of Highway 9, follow Albion Trail for a few metres until you come to a driveway numbered 17000. Turn right here and look for a small sign for the Oak Ridges Trail. The sign is white with green lettering.

23. Follow the Oak Ridges Trail and its white blazes heading at about a 45-degree angle away from Highway 9. This is the unopened road allowance for Hunsden Road. Stay to the left of the driveway. The trail gets overgrown in parts, so watch for the green blazes. Also, keep your dog on leash as there are a number of warnings about guard dogs here.

24. At the first trail intersection you come to veer right staying on the larger trail. In the forest, there is a sea of trilliums. It must be gorgeous in the spring. It can be confusing in this area – keep to the right of the various trail Y-intersections, next to the "No Trespassing" signs and near the fence on your right. Look for the white blazes.

25. When you leave this forested area, you come to some open fields. A line of mature trees continues on your right. The trail goes straight ahead following this line of trees. Keep going straight, following alongside the line of mature trees. The Oak Ridges Trail Association needs to be a bit more generous with their white blazes through this section. Don't panic if you don't see any blazes for a bit.

26. The Oak Ridges Moraine, which stretches for 160k from the Niagara Escarpment in the west to the Trent River system in the east, is about 13k

Catalogue house.

wide on average. Its gravelly soils play a vital role in cleaning the water throughout Southern Ontario.

27. Look through the tree line to your right to see the sparkling blue water of a large quarry pond.

28. Continue following the white blazes and the fence line of this quarry that is marked with large blocks.

29. Cross over a fallen-down piece of snow fence and the Churchill Baptist Church should come into view.

30. Walk through the churchyard, cross Mount Wolfe Road and follow Hunsden Side Road for 1.6k. You pass by some lovely houses on this quiet road.

31. At Mount Pleasant Road, turn right until you cross the active railway tracks and return to your car. Just before the railway tracks is a "catalogue" house. About 100 years ago, it was ordered from a catalogue, perhaps Eaton's. It arrived at this location in pieces via what is now the Caledon Trailway but was the Hamilton & Northwestern Railway at the time, and was assembled at this location.

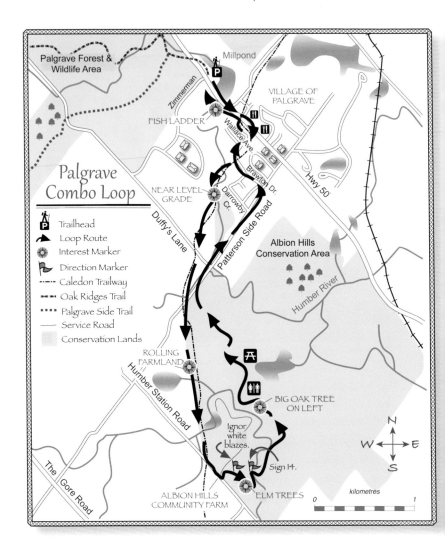

Millpond

Palgrave Forest &
Wildlife Area

VILLAGE OF
PALGRAVE

Zimmerman

FISH LADDER

Wallace Ave.

Brawton Dr.

Hwy 50

Palgrave
Combo Loop

NEAR LEVEL
GRADE

Darrowby
Cr.

Patterson Side Road

Albion Hills
Conservation Area

Duffy's Lane

Humber River

P   Trailhead

Loop Route

Interest Marker

Direction Marker

—·—·— Caledon Trailway

━··━ Oak Ridges Trail

•••••• Palgrave Side Trail

———— Service Road

Conservation Lands

ROLLING
FARMLAND

Humber Station Road

BIG OAK TREE
ON LEFT

Ignor
white
blazes.

N
W   E
S

The Gore Road

Sign 14.

ALBION HILLS
COMMUNITY FARM

ELM TREES

kilometres
0   1

*"Happy is the man who has
acquired the love of walking for its own sake!"*

W.J. HOLLAND

Palgrave Combo Loop

OVERVIEW

The more I hiked around Palgrave, the more loops I put together. The Albion Hills Conservation Area, the Palgrave Forest and Wildlife Area, and the Caledon Trailway are all in the vicinity of this small village, which makes for great hiking. When you add the considerable contributions of the Palgrave Rotary Club for infrastructure, the experience is even better.

This 11k loop passes through Palgrave on both the outward and return journeys so you see lots of the village and have two chances to stop for a coffee and a bite to eat. Frequent the new (2014) Church pub, if it's open. The route takes you through the Oak Ridges Moraine's rolling landscape, before dropping deep into the forested Albion Hills Conservation Area. It also passes by Palgrave's fishway, dam and millpond.

As part of this route is in the Albion Hills Conservation Area, I encourage you to stop by the gate and pay the fee. Ontario's conservation authorities do a great deal to protect the environment and provide fabulous recreational opportunities. For instance, the network of trails you will be walking on is extensive and well maintained. These things are expensive and users' fees help offset the cost.

Directions

1. Park in the Palgrave Rotary Parking Lot on the east side of Highway 50, just past the bridge north of Palgrave.

2. Look for the plaque in the parking area that describes the Humber River in English, French and Anishnawbe, the language spoken by First Nations in this area. The Humber River's name means "gathering place to tie up" and was part of the Carrying Place Trail, a main transportation route between Lake Ontario and Huronia in times past.

3. Leave the Rotary Parking Lot and follow the trail that heads south toward Palgrave. You will pass by the large millpond that is a skating rink in the winter and a fishing hole in the summer. A fisherman there told me he'd recently caught a 2½-lb bass. This is part of the Humber River.

4. The trail goes under Highway 50 and crosses the dam that keeps the millpond a pond. This is the site of a sawmill built in the 1850s. It was replaced by a flour and gristmill that was closed in 1968. Just past the bridge there is a spillway built especially to let fish get around the dam.

5. Continue on Highway 50 entering the village. Palgrave or Buckstown is a pretty village (despite being intersected by a highway) and the former home to David Milne, a well-known Canadian painter. Back in the late 1800s, the arrival of the Hamilton & Northwestern Railway helped Palgrave grow. Dennis "Buck" Dolan, the tavern owner, was an avid deer hunter. It was his prowess that resulted in the village being known as Buckstown. Palgrave is also home to the Caledon Equestrian Park where the world's greatest show jumpers put on an exciting show.

6. Continue walking south on Highway 50 past the gas station. Just ahead is a large, grapevine-covered trellis that marks the Trans Canada Trail as it follows the Caledon Trailway. Turn right going under the trellis and then past an open-air pavilion with signs that say "Palgrave."

7. The Caledon Trailway passes over Brawton Drive before crossing the rolling landscape of the Oak Ridges Moraine. Just after you leave the village, this old railway line spans a deep ravine. Notice how they filled the ravine to level the grade. It's frightening to think of the work it would have entailed.

8. About 1.5k from the trellis, you travel over Duffy's Lane on an overpass. Continue on the Caledon Trailway for another 2k, crossing Patterson Side Road and arriving at Humber Station Road. Rail trails are a bit flat for my

Stay on the trail passing by these elms.

taste, but they are great when you walk with a friend or friends and want to have a good gab because they are wide and you can travel abreast.

9. Turn left on Humber Station Road and then, after only 250m, you come to the back entrance to the Albion Hills Conservation Area. In 2014, there was a sign that said Albion Hills Community Farm. Turn left and follow this road. There is a NO ACCESS sign as well. As you are on the trail, you can enter, but I encourage you to either buy an annual pass or pay at the main gate.

10. A short 100m later, the trail leaves the road at about a 45-degree angle, heading to the right across a field. In the distance you can see a post with a white blaze marking the Humber Valley Heritage Trail. Follow this trail.

11. In another 250m, you come to a post on your left that has white blazes that indicate you should leave the obvious trail and turn left. DO NOT leave the trail, keep walking straight ahead past a pair of elm trees still alive in 2014. In 1967, Dutch Elm Disease began killing Ontario's magnificent elms. I can still recall large areas of tree carcasses, and how close my dad came to tears

when he had to cut one down near our house. Some elms survived because they were naturally immune. Others survived because they were far enough away from infected ones that the European elm bark beetle that carries the ailment couldn't reach them.

12. Pass the elms as the trail skirts the side of a field. The trail turns sharply to the left almost doubling back on itself. It goes down a gentle slope and into the forest. Look for Sign 14. Turn right here and go over the wooden bridge.

13. Stick to this well-marked and well-used trail until you come to a junction where the Sugar Rush mountain-biking trail exits to your left. It is at the top of a long climb. Turn left just past the Sugar Rush trail and follow the Blue Trail where you will see a blue arrow at Sign 16. Keep an eye open for mountain bikes on these trails.

14. Stick with the blue arrows as the route continues through the woods and then enters an open area with picnic tables, washrooms, tap water and a parking lot. Cross a small road at Sign 26 and eventually arrive at Sign 34, about 2k after the Sugar Rush trail.

15. At Sign 34, leave the Blue Trail and connect with the Red Trail at Sign 33. It is straight ahead of you.

16. At Sign 35, leave the Red Trail by turning left on to the Yellow Trail. When you see the sign for the Tea Cup mountain biking trail, turn left again. This trail takes you out of the Albion Hills Conservation Area and on to the Caledon Trailway.

17. Turn right on to the Caledon Trailway and then immediately right again on to Patterson Side Road.

18. Follow Patterson Side Road for about 1k, crossing Duffy's Lane en route.

19. Turn left on to Brawton Drive, cross the Caledon Trailway, and follow Brawton to Wallace Avenue.

20. Turn left on to Wallace Avenue where you will enter the older part of Palgrave. Note how much smaller the older houses tend to be.

21. Follow Wallace Avenue until it turns right and becomes Church Street.

22. Follow Church Street until it pops out on to Highway 50 not far from the Palgrave Variety, the Palgrave Café (closed Sundays) and The Church pub. Visit them as your stomach, timing and pocketbook allow.

23. From Church Street you have less than 600m to walk on Highway 50 until you come to the Palgrave Rotary Club parking lot and your car.

Palgrave Forest Humber Loop

Nicola's
Insider Info

LENGTH
9.6 kilometres

LEVEL OF DIFFICULTY
Easy

LENGTH OF TIME
2.5 to 3.5 hours

NUMBER OF STEPS
13,010

kCAL BURNED 405

HIGHLIGHTS
Ferns, Eastern hemlocks, black cherries

PLACES TO EAT/DRINK
None en route. Palgrave is close by: Palgrave Café (closed Sundays), Palgrave Variety Store, The Church pub (Wed to Sun, 4pm to 12pm)

ENTRANCE FEE
n/a

OVERVIEW

This hike was new territory for me when I walked it, which is always exciting. There's a tendency to complete the same routes over and over again because you know them and it's easy, so it was great to have a surprise around every corner.

Much of the route goes through the Palgrave Forest and Wildlife Area, a 306-hectare tract of land owned and managed by the Toronto and Region Conservation Authority. It is home to 200 species of plants and animals.

There isn't really a destination on this hike. Instead it wanders casually through lovely forests, across wetlands and along some beautiful country roads. It offers the best features of the Oak Ridges Moraine: rolling hills, sandy soil, vistas and interesting plants and trees. There were fabulous ferns, and I came across the prettiest grove of lacy Eastern hemlocks and big fat old black cherry trees.

The trail is mostly flat and often on a double track. There were a few places, especially near the end, where it looked as if the trail was well used by mountain bikes, so keep an eye and ear out for approaching bicycles.

GPS

TRAIL MARKER
Loop 30

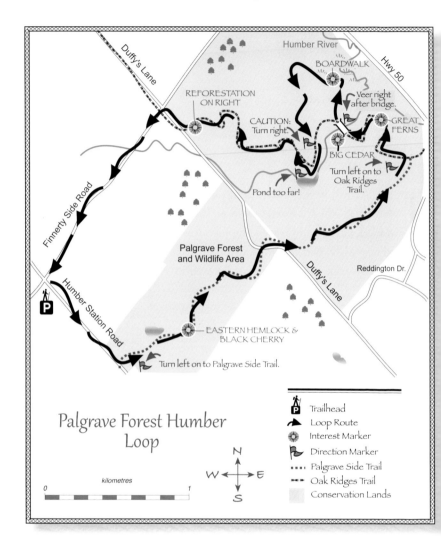

Duffy's Lane

Humber River

Hwy 50

BOARDWALK

Veer right
after bridge.

REFORESTATION
ON RIGHT

CAUTION:
Turn right.

GREAT
FERNS

BIG CEDAR

Turn left on to
Oak Ridges
Trail.

Finnerty Side Road

Pond too far!

Palgrave Forest
and Wildlife Area

Duffy's Lane

Reddington Dr.

Humber Station Road

EASTERN HEMLOCK &
BLACK CHERRY

Turn left on to Palgrave Side Trail.

Palgrave Forest Humber Loop

Trailhead
Loop Route
Interest Marker
Direction Marker
Palgrave Side Trail
Oak Ridges Trail
Conservation Lands

kilometres

0   1

N
W   E
S

*"Some people like to make a little garden out of life
and walk down a path."*

JEAN ANOUILH

High density birdhouses.

Directions

1. Park at the corner of Humber Station Road and Finnerty Side Road. There are wide shoulders on both roads.

2. Walk south on Humber Station Road past some lovely homes.

3. After 850m, there is a big sign for the Palgrave Forest and Wildlife Area. There is a smaller blue sign noting this is also the Palgrave Side Trail of the Bruce Trail. Turn left here leaving Humber Station Road.

4. Follow the wide double track toward the forest. It is marked by the Palgrave Side Trail's blue blazes.

5. You pass by a pond on your left and enter a forest where there are some lovely lacy Eastern hemlocks and large black cherry trees. The latter have very black scaly bark. (*See photo on page 25.*)

6. About 1.5k after leaving Humber Station Road you come to Duffy's Lane. The Duffy family was one of the first families to settle in Albion, and Eliza Duffy was one of the first Methodist preachers in the area. The original Duffy homestead near Bolton is a designated heritage site.

7. Cross Duffy's Lane. Enter the forest on the other side of the road and follow the blue blazes of the Palgrave Side Trail along a wide flat trail. There is some nice open terrain here.

8. About 1.2k later you arrive at a trail junction marked with a wooden sign #10. The Oak Ridges Trail turns left here and so do you. You leave the Bruce Trail's blue blazes and follow the Oak Ridges Trail's white blazes. The Oak Ridges Trail is not as well marked as the Bruce Trail so don't panic if there are gaps between white blazes.

9. Turn right at Sign 13 and keep following the white blazes. You come upon an area where there are lovely ferns. I spotted bracken ferns, ostrich ferns, standard ferns and more.

10. You come to another trail junction. This time there is a massive white cedar on your right. You see the back of Sign 14 on your left. Turn right here.

11. You cross a wooden bridge and come across a bench where you can take a break.

12. After the bridge veer right at Sign 15.

13. About 300m after the bridge, turn left on to a boardwalk over a wetland.

14. The trail meanders through scrub brush until, about 1k later, you come to a T-intersection. On your left will be the back of Sign 16. CAUTION: The white blazes here tell you to turn left, but you should turn right. So turn right. Otherwise you end up back at Sign 15.

15. Less than 200m later you arrive at a small pond. There was a family of small ducks swimming when I was there. If you are looking at the pond, you have gone too far. Backtrack about 20m looking for Sign 17 (on your left if you are returning from the pond or on your right if you didn't get as far as the pond). Follow the trail into the forest here.

16. Some 250m later, you come to a fork in the trail. Both paths are well used and neither has a white marker. Take the left fork.

17. You leave the forest. Keep your eyes and ears open for mountain bikers.

18. Turn left at Sign 18.

19. Turn left at Sign 19. There is an excellent view of the area from the top of the hill.

20. You come up to a small dirt road. This is Duffy's Lane. Follow alongside it until there is an opening in the fence on your left.

21. Leave the trail here picking up and turning right on to Duffy's Lane.

22. After a gentle rise in the road, you come to Finnerty Side Road. Turn left here.

23. Walk along Finnerty Side Road for 1.5k until you return to your vehicle.

Palgrave
Village Loop

OVERVIEW

This is a great village loop that combines a walk through the forest, a latte in Palgrave, a stroll along the Caledon Trailway and a meander along a peaceful country road.

The village of Palgrave has done a great job of developing its millpond, which becomes a huge skating rink in the winter thanks to Ken Hunt, the village's Ice Angel. He does the required snow removal. The Oak Ridges Trail takes you right through the village and en route you pass through the Palgrave Rotary Park. This branch of the Rotary Club is very active and has funded some wonderful community works including washrooms and benches at the skating rink.

Another Palgrave feature is the Caledon Equestrian Park on the east end of the village. Host site for the equestrian events of the 2015 Pan Am Games, it is the province's premier show-jumping facility where North America's best come to compete.

Enjoy this great combo hike.

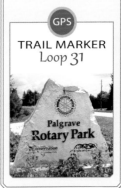

GPS

TRAIL MARKER
Loop 31

Palgrave
Rotary Park

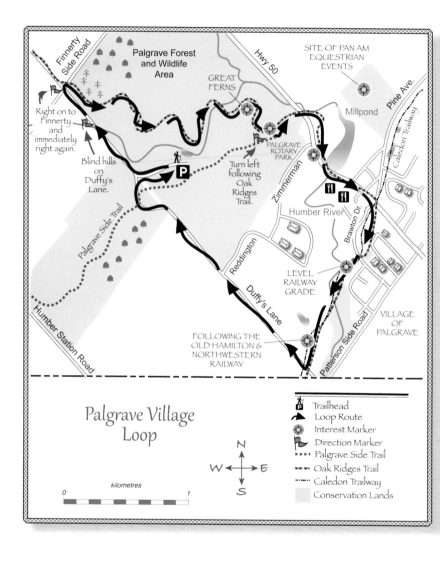

Finnerty Side Road

Palgrave Forest
and Wildlife
Area

Hwy 50

SITE OF PAN AM
EQUESTRIAN
EVENTS

GREAT
FERNS

Pine Ave.

Millpond

Caledon Trailway

Right on to
Finnerty
and
immediately
right again.

PALGRAVE
ROTARY
PARK

Blind hills
on
Duffy's
Lane.

P

Turn left
following
Oak
Ridges
Trail.

Zimmerman

Humber River

Brawton Dr.

Palgrave Side Trail

Reddington

LEVEL
RAILWAY
GRADE

VILLAGE
OF
PALGRAVE

Duffy's Lane

Humber Station Road

FOLLOWING THE
OLD HAMILTON &
NORTHWESTERN
RAILWAY

Patterson Side Road

Palgrave Village Loop

kilometres

0   1

N
W — E
S

🚩 Trailhead
➤ Loop Route
✺ Interest Marker
🚩 Direction Marker
••••• Palgrave Side Trail
—•—• Oak Ridges Trail
—••— Caledon Trailway
⬜ Conservation Lands

*"Walking is good for solving problems –
it's like the feet are little psychiatrists."*

PEPPER GIARDINO

Directions

1. Park in the lot in the Palgrave Forest and Wildlife Area (formerly Palgrave Conservation Area). It is accessible from Duffy's Lane between Patterson Side Road and Finnerty Side Road. Note that Duffy's Lane is not serviced in winter north of the parking lot so you can only access it from the south at that time.

2. From the parking lot walk toward Duffy's Lane and turn right. While Duffy's Lane is a quiet country road without many cars, it has some blind hills. Keep your ears open for cars and stay as far off the road as possible given the narrow shoulders. In other words, take care along this short stretch of road.

3. Turn right on to Finnerty Side Road and then immediately right again on to the Oak Ridges Trail where you see the signs for the trail. Follow the white blazes into the reforested area going straight ahead and walking parallel but in the opposite direction, to where you just walked on Duffy's Lane.

4. Follow the Oak Ridges Trail and its white blazes as it winds its way through the Palgrave Forest and Wildlife Area. You will walk through old forest, reforest and wet areas as the landscape changes. Be aware that mountain bikers use this trail so keep your eyes and ears open. I only saw two cyclists as I walked it and they were both polite and slowed down, but there are a few blind hills so be mindful.

5. There are a number of signposts along this section marking trails in the Palgrave Forest and Wildlife Area. It might help to know where you go at each signpost so here is a list for reference purposes:

▲	19	straight	▶	15	right at bench and cross bridge
▲	18	straight	◀	14	left
◀	17	left	◀	13	left
▲	16	straight	◀	10	left

6. Some 3k from the start of your hike, you arrive at the junction between the Oak Ridges Trail and the Palgrave Side Trail (Sign 10). The Palgrave Side Trail begins here though you will NOT take it. Turn left continuing to follow the Oak Ridges Trail and its white blazes.

7. Soon you arrive at Highway 50. Cross it with caution and turn right on the far side. At the end of the guardrail, the Oak Ridges Trail leaves Highway 50 to the left and follows a wire fence.

8. In 400m, you come to the Palgrave Rotary Park where there is a parking lot and information sign. Continue through the parking area until you come to the large millpond. This millpond is the result of a dam on the Humber River. Each winter, Palgrave's "Ice Angel," Ken Hunt, maintains the ice rinks. He began the practice when he couldn't find another venue where his children could skate. The rinks are open to anyone who wants to use them at their own risk. There are benches and washrooms paid for, in part, by the Palgrave Rotary Club. There are hockey tournaments and other events held on the ice that make the winter a much more enjoyable season for many "Palgravians."

9. The trail goes under Highway 50 and then you cross over the dam on a metal walkway. While on the walkway over the dam look downstream and to your left. There is a stream that enters the river below the dam. This is a fishway that allows our finned friends to get around the dam. Trout Unlimited Canada has been monitoring the effectiveness of the fishway, but no results are currently available.

10. The trail climbs back on to Highway 50 and heads into the village.

11. Palgrave or Buckstown is a pretty village (despite being intersected by a highway) and the former home of David Milne, a well-known Canadian painter who lived there in the 1930s. Back in the late 1800s, it was the arrival of the Hamilton & Northwestern Railway (now Caledon Trailway) that helped Palgrave grow. Dennis "Buck" Dolan, the tavern owner, was an avid deer hunter. His prowess resulted in the village being known as Buckstown for many years.

12. Look for the Palgrave Café (closed Sundays), Palgrave Variety and The Church pub. The café serves lunch, lattes and other great coffees. Where else but in Caledon can you get a latte while walking a route almost entirely through the forest? Unfortunately, when I arrived the café was closed so I picked up "provisions" in the variety store. Palgrave also has a community kitchen. A Peel Health-certified facility, it can be rented by anyone needing to use a commercial kitchen.

13. Continue walking along Highway 50 past the gas station until you come to the Caledon Trailway. Follow the Trailway to the right as it passes under a trellis covered in grapevines. A few metres down the path there are benches and a pavilion where I sat and ate my snacks. The Caledon Trailway follows the route of the Hamilton & Northwestern Railway that ran from Hamilton

to Collingwood. Emil Kolb, a Caledon resident and long-time chairman of the Region of Peel, was key in the Caledon Trailway's birth. He cast the deciding vote when the decision was made to return the right-of-way to property owners or turn it into a public trail. He contributed to the Foreword of this guide.

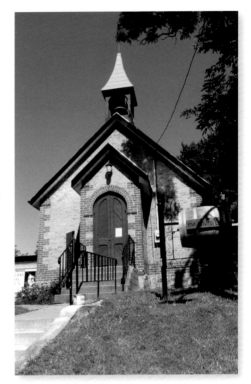

The Church pub in Palgrave.

14. Follow the Caledon Trailway crossing Brawton Drive until you come to the bridge that goes over Duffy's Lane. You leave the Caledon Trailway and the Oak Ridges Trail here. There is a path on the left as you approach the bridge that goes down the slope to the road. The distance between the trellis and Duffy's Lane is 1.5k.

15. Turn right and walk north on Duffy's Lane. Practically underneath the overpass is a large sign for Deerfields Stables Country Inn. This "Private Club" is now a retreat centre that specializes in managing the biological aging process. Yikes! Its best feature, in my opinion however, is its Gypsy vanner horses. These black and white darlings are a sight with their long flowing manes and tails, and feathery legs.

16. Continue walking north on Duffy's Lane as it winds its way up and down some steepish hills. It's a lovely little road that is partially closed during the winter. Stay on the shoulder to be safe.

17. After walking for a little more than 2k along Duffy's Lane, you return to the entrance to the parking lot. Turn right here and find your vehicle.

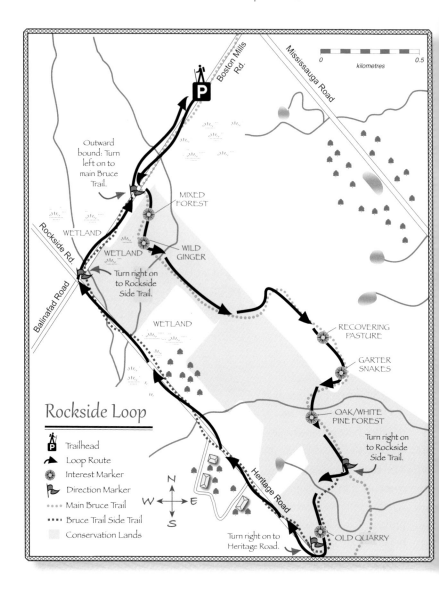

Boston Mills Rd.

Mississauga Road

0   kilometres   0.5

Outward bound: Turn left on to main Bruce Trail.

MIXED FOREST

Rockside Rd.

WETLAND

Balinafad Road

WETLAND

WILD GINGER

Turn right on to Rockside Side Trail.

WETLAND

RECOVERING PASTURE

GARTER SNAKES

OAK/WHITE PINE FOREST

Turn right on to Rockside Side Trail.

Rockside Loop

- 🚶 Trailhead
- ➤ Loop Route
- ✺ Interest Marker
- ⚑ Direction Marker
- ⋯ Main Bruce Trail
- ▪▪▪ Bruce Trail Side Trail
- ▨ Conservation Lands

N
W   E
S

Heritage Road

Turn right on to Heritage Road.

OLD QUARRY

*A dog is one of the remaining reasons
why some people can be persuaded to go for a walk.*

O.A. BATTISTA

Rockside Loop

OVERVIEW

I want to start the overview for every hike with the words, "I love," but I really do love this loop. It packs so much into 6k. Over the distance you are almost entirely on your own except for the odd garter snake and the cutest little American toads. At first you are buried in a seemingly perfect mixed forest where there are maples, black cherries, ashes and birch trees so white you will think they are advertisements for toothpaste. You emerge into the sunshine passing through recuperating farm fields before entering a forest that is altogether different with oaks, white pines and cedars.

You walk by a handful of houses buried in the trees where you might think: What a lovely private spot to have a home. And when your hike is done you are steps away from the Terra Cotta Inn & Pub or Spirit Tree Estate Cidery where treats await: thin crust pizza made in a wood-burning oven, artisanal bread, homemade soups, cappuccino and, of course, a variety of hard and sweet cider made from homegrown apples.

Thanks to the Bruce Trail volunteers who worked hard on this trail, cleaning the debris resulting from the devastating ice storm in December 2013.

This route is generously sponsored by
*Spirit Tree Estate Cidery (**SpiritTreeCider.com**).*

Nicola's
Insider Info

LENGTH
5.9 kilometres

LEVEL OF DIFFICULTY
Moderate

LENGTH OF TIME
1.5 to 2 hours

NUMBER OF STEPS
8,264

kCAL BURNED 267

HIGHLIGHTS
Beautiful forests, lovely homes, old quarry, Spirit Tree Estate Cidery

PLACES TO EAT/DRINK
Spirit Tree Estate Cidery, Terra Cotta Inn & Pub

ENTRANCE FEE
n/a

TRAIL MARKER
Loop 32

Any day is a good day for a walk in the woods.

Directions

1. Park near the dead end of Boston Mills Road on the west side of Mississauga Road. The road is quiet and wide. The trailhead is here.

2. Leave your car and continue west on the road passing by the sign that says "Private Road." This is the access to the Bruce Trail. Please respect the property owner by only walking on the driveway until the Bruce Trail begins.

3. Follow the white blazes of the Bruce Trail into the forest.

4. The trail climbs a bit before dropping down into a swampy area. A short 500m from where you entered the forest, you come to a spot where the main Bruce Trail turns a sharp left and the Rockside Side Trail goes straight. Turn left here following the white blazes of the main Bruce Trail. WATCH CAREFULLY FOR THIS TURNOFF. IT IS EASY TO MISS.

5. You enter a wonderful mixed forest featuring sugar maples interspersed with black cherry, beech, hophornbeam (ironwood), ash and even an occasional Eastern hemlock. Look for wild ginger as well.

6. After a time, the forest opens into a recovering pasture, likely once used to graze cattle. Note how the apple and thorn trees are starting to take over now there is no livestock.

7. Soon you are surrounded by a different forest consisting of oaks, white pines and Eastern white cedars. I was startled by two big fat Eastern garter snakes (*Thamnophis sirtalis*) near here. They almost always have three yellow stripes, are not poisonous and are unique in that females give birth to live young rather than lay eggs.

8. About 2.5k after the sharp left turn, you come to the Rockside Side Trail. Turn right following its blue blazes. Soon after you turn, you come to a lovely bridge over the quintessential babbling brook.

9. Some time later, but just before you come to Heritage Road, you pass by big piles of stones camouflaged by vegetation. They indicate there was once a quarry here.

10. When you come to a road, turn right, following it. This is Heritage Road and it is very quiet.

11. Heritage Road narrows and the pavement ends as you pass by several lovely houses buried in the maple forest. The trail becomes a track. You are still following the Rockside Side Trail with its blue blazes.

12. Follow this arrow-straight route for about 1.5k until you come to a corner where the Ballinafad Road turns 90 degrees to become Rockside Road.

13. Turn sharp right, following the Rockside Side Trail blue blazes at this intersection of roads. You walk onto the road and then immediately off it again onto the trail. Look for wildlife or perhaps frogs or salamanders as you pass by some large ponds in this wetland area.

14. About 1k later you are back at your car.

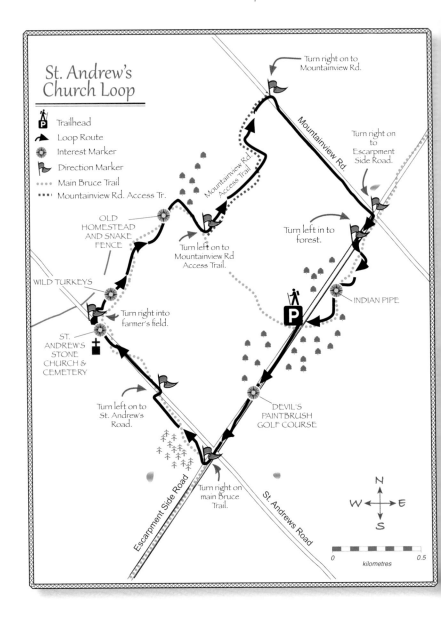

St. Andrew's Church Loop

P   Trailhead
▲   Loop Route
✳   Interest Marker
⚑   Direction Marker
••••   Main Bruce Trail
▪▪▪▪   Mountainview Rd. Access Tr.

Turn right on to Mountainview Rd.

Mountainview Rd.

Turn right on to Escarpment Side Road.

Mountainview Rd. Access Trail

Turn left in to forest.

OLD HOMESTEAD AND SNAKE FENCE

Turn left on to Mountainview Rd Access Trail.

INDIAN PIPE

WILD TURKEYS

Turn right into farmer's field.

ST. ANDREW'S STONE CHURCH & CEMETERY

Turn left on to St. Andrew's Road.

DEVIL'S PAINTBRUSH GOLF COURSE

Turn right on main Bruce Trail.

Escarpment Side Road

St. Andrews Road

N
W   E
S

0   kilometres   0.5

*"I see my path, but I don't know where it leads.
Not knowing where I'm going is what inspires me to travel it."*

ROSALIA DE CASTRO

St. Andrew's Church Loop

OVERVIEW

Visiting the precious St. Andrew's Stone Church and its cemetery are reason enough to hike this route, but you get to walk across some lovely farms and through peaceful forest too. Many of Caledon's hikes are in the woods or across meadows so it's a nice change to see working agricultural land. Just after you pass by St. Andrew's Stone Church, the trail leaves the road and enters a farm field where an explosion of about a dozen wild turkeys announced my arrival – a sure sign of Ontario's success in reintroducing these awkward birds. Farther along, I walked beside a long line of big old shady maple trees among which a split-rail fence snaked its way. Odd I thought. Then I came out into an open area surrounded on four sides by big mature trees. I realized a farmhouse must have been here once.

In the forest there was evidence of spring ephemeral flowers, so consider walking this route in May. I saw a big patch of bloodroot, a plant that "bleeds" and has a great Latin name: *Sanguinaria canadensis*.

33

Nicola's
Insider Info

LENGTH
5.2 kilometres

LEVEL OF DIFFICULTY
Easy

LENGTH OF TIME
1.25 to 1.75 hours

NUMBER OF STEPS
7,088

kCAL BURNED 235

HIGHLIGHTS
Old farmstead and farmland, St. Andrew's Stone Church and cemetery, Indian pipe, bloodroot

PLACES TO EAT/DRINK
Nothing en route. In nearby Caledon East: Gabe's Country Bake Shoppe, Caledon Hills Coffee Company, Gourmandissimo, Prime Beef Bistro and more

ENTRANCE FEE
n/a

GPS

TRAIL MARKER
Loop 33

ST. ANDREWS

Directions

1. Park on Escarpment Side Road between St. Andrew's Road and Mountainview Road where the main Bruce Trail enters the forest to the south. There are two spots where this happens, park near the more western entrance as there is more room on the shoulder for your vehicle.

2. Walk west on Escarpment Side Road toward St. Andrew's Road. Note that on your left there is a links-style golf course. It's called the Devil's Paintbrush and differs in a nice way from most golf courses, which are fertilized and "pesticized" and mowed to a point the fairways look more like AstroTurf than grass.

3. Cross St. Andrew's Road and climb up a small rise. At the top, there is a sign for the main Bruce Trail on the right side of Escarpment Side Road. Turn right here, entering the forest.

4. Follow this trail through a reforested area as it keeps you off the road. After 500m, the trail returns to the road.

5. Turn left on to St. Andrew's Road. Just ahead you come to the lovely St. Andrew's Stone Church, built in 1853. Wander around the cemetery as it has lots of old gravestones, most bearing the names of the Scottish, Irish and English immigrants who pioneered this part of Ontario.

6. Return to the road and keep heading north. A short 200m past the church, the trail leaves the road and turns sharply right. This is marked by the Bruce Trail's white blazes. This is where I scared up a family of at least a dozen wild turkeys. Flocks of these big awkward birds are now a common sight in these parts – the result of a reintroduction program started in 1984.

7. Follow the trail as it passes by a horse pasture. If you look to your left and back toward St. Andrew's Road, you can see the bright red roof of a new house in front of an old barn and stone farmhouse across the road. This is Caledon in 2015: New and old.

8. Farther along this stretch, you walk beside a long line of shady old maple trees. In between them snakes a split-rail fence. These fences were favoured because they are self-supporting and therefore don't require you to dig post holes in the rocky soils found in this part of Caledon. On the downside, they take a lot of split rails. Cedar is the preferred material for these rails because it is naturally more resistant to rot than most wood.

9. As I admired the tree line and fence, I wondered what it was doing here in the middle of nowhere. Then I walked into an open area bordered on

Snake fence.

four sides by straight lines of mature trees. I realized there must have been a farmhouse here once. If I'd rooted around, I may have found some old perennial plants left over from the gardens.

10. About 700m after leaving St. Andrew's Road, the trail turns a sharp right. Then, 200m later, you come to the Mountainview Road Access Trail. It heads off across a field to your left in a straight line of blue blazes. Take this side trail leaving the main Bruce Trail behind.

11. Less than 1k later, the trail leads you to a short set of stairs and on to Mountainview Road. Turn right and walk along this quiet country road until you come to Escarpment Side Road, about 750m later. There are no blazes along this stretch of road.

12. Turn right on Escarpment Side Road where you pick up the white blazes of the main Bruce Trail again. Just ahead look for where the trail turns left and enters the forest.

13. Turn left and enter a mostly maple woods that is a nice change if you are walking on a hot sunny day. I came across some Indian pipe (*Monotropa uniflora*) here. This white parasitic plant grows in the dark forest because it doesn't need sunlight to produce chlorophyll. Instead, it feeds on nearby trees.

14. The trail comes back on to Escarpment Side Road where your car is parked.

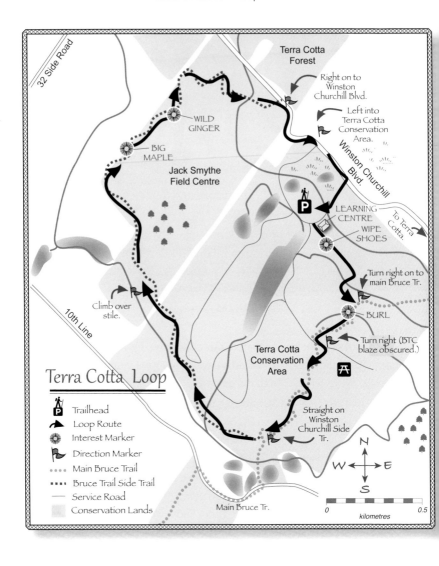

Terra Cotta Forest

Right on to Winston Churchill Blvd.

Left into Terra Cotta Conservation Area.

Winston Churchill Blvd.

To Terra Cotta.

WILD GINGER

BIG MAPLE

Jack Smythe Field Centre

32 Side Road

P

LEARNING CENTRE

WIPE SHOES

Turn right on to main Bruce Tr.

BURL

Turn right (BTC blaze obscured.)

Climb over stile.

10th Line

Terra Cotta Loop

🏕 Trailhead
➤ Loop Route
✷ Interest Marker
🚩 Direction Marker
···· Main Bruce Trail
▪▪▪▪ Bruce Trail Side Trail
— Service Road
▨ Conservation Lands

Terra Cotta Conservation Area

Straight on Winston Churchill Side Tr.

Main Bruce Tr.

N
W — E
S

0   kilometres   0.5

"He who limps is still walking."

STANISLAW J. LEC

Terra Cotta Loop

34

Nicola's
Insider Info

LENGTH
5.7 kilometres

LEVEL OF DIFFICULTY
Moderate

LENGTH OF TIME
1.5 to 2 hours

NUMBER OF STEPS
7,972

kCAL BURNED 258

HIGHLIGHTS
Big old beech trees,
shagbark hickory, Terra
Cotta Inn Pub, all-trail
route, Tour de Terra
Cotta cycling race first
weekend in August

PLACES TO EAT/DRINK
Terra Cotta Country
Store has cold drinks and
frozen yoghurt. Terra
Cotta Inn & Pub

ENTRANCE FEE
Adults $5/children &
seniors $3 (cash only)

OVERVIEW

The Japanese believe time spent walking in the forest isn't just good for your body; it's good for your soul too. At last count, Japan had created 48 Forest Therapy Trails. Well, this hike is definitely healthy since it is almost entirely within a mixed hardwood forest.

It is within the Terra Cotta Conservation Area and the neighbouring Jack Smythe Field Centre in Caledon's southwest corner. As a result, you will see some trees that don't grow elsewhere in Caledon. There are shagbark hickories, for example. Keep your eyes open for this Carolinian species as well as some grand dame maple trees.

Limestone comes to the surface along with red clay near Terra Cotta, once known as Salmonville because of the great fishing here. The Union Presbyterian Church and the "fifth line" schoolhouse on Terra Cotta's south side were both made from local rock. History books claim Terra Cotta's quarries supplied stone for Toronto's old City Hall, the Timothy Eaton Memorial Church, Queen's Park, Hart House, the Soldier's Tower and Union Station's pillars.

GPS

TRAIL MARKER
Loop 34

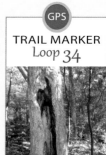

Directions

1. Park in the Terra Cotta Conservation Area. The entrance is on Winston Churchill Blvd., 2k north of King Street and the village of Terra Cotta.

2. Follow the signs to the Watershed Learning Centre.

3. Go past the right-hand side of the Learning Centre and look for the Vaughan Trail and its orange markers. Follow it. This trail is also the A. F. Coventry Nature Trail with yellow markers. When I walked this trail, there was a gadget that cleans your shoes. Please use it. Many invasive species are spread by hikers who pick seeds up in their treads. This is particularly true for garlic mustard.

4. Soon you cross over a wooden bridge and come to a trail junction with the main Bruce Trail. Turn right here following the white blazes of the Bruce Trail. You are still on the Vaughan Trail as well. Just after you turn, there is a great burl on an oak tree. Burls are tree growths wherein the grain of the tree is deformed. They are caused by some form of stress such as disease or injury. Wood turners often make fabulous bowls from burls.

5. You come to a T-intersection where you turn left following both the Bruce Trail (white blazes) and the Vaughan Trail (orange markers) on a service road.

6. A short 60m later, turn right following the Vaughan Trail. The Bruce Trail turns here too but the blazes are sometimes covered by vegetation. Look for the "Trees 2000" sign as well.

7. After about 200m, you come to a spot where the Vaughan Trail leaves the main Bruce Trail. Go straight, following the main Bruce Trail and its white markers.

8. After another 300m, you arrive at another trail junction. This is where you pick up the Winston Churchill Side Trail. Turn right on to the Winston Churchill Side Trail following blue blazes. At this intersection, you will see a sign telling you that if you go straight you will leave the conservation area. The Winston Churchill Side Trail passes through the Jack Smythe Field Centre, an educational facility owned by the Peel Board of Education.

9. After about 3k, the Winston Churchill Side Trail arrives at Winston Churchill Blvd. and ends. Along the way, look for big American beech trees with their smooth, light grey bark; hophornbeams with their peeling bark and wild ginger. Hophornbeam is a "common" name for *Ostrya virginiana*. This is the only species of Ostrya that is native to Canada. It is slow-growing, long-

A juvenile American toad.

lived (150 years) and of little commercial value. Despite looking nothing like blue-beech (a member of the birch family and not the American beech mentioned above), hophornbeams are sometimes confused with the former because they both go by the common name ironwood. This name reflects the hardness of the wood of both trees. The name hophornbeam is thought to be derived from "hop" because their fruit clusters look a lot like hops used to make beer, "horn" to reflect the hardness of the wood and "beam," which is an archaic word for tree.

10. You climb over a stile along this great stretch of trail. Be sure to stay on the Winston Churchill Side Trail and its blue blazes until you come to the road. Don't be put off by the "No Trespassing" signs. Hikers are welcome. The signs are meant to keep you from wandering off the trail

11. Turn right on Winston Churchill Blvd. and walk down the hill toward Terra Cotta. When I was young, the wetland you pass by on your right at the bottom of the hill was a swimming area complete with a clay-bottom pond, colourful buoys and, best of all, a concession stand. Once a summer, Mum would take my four siblings and me there for the day. The water was much warmer than the Credit River (and suspiciously murky) and we'd be able to buy a pack of candy cigarettes or sweet tarts or other sugary delight. It was bliss.

12. After about 500m, turn right into the Terra Cotta Conservation Area where you will find your car. While walking down the hill, it's safer to walk on the outside of the blind corners.

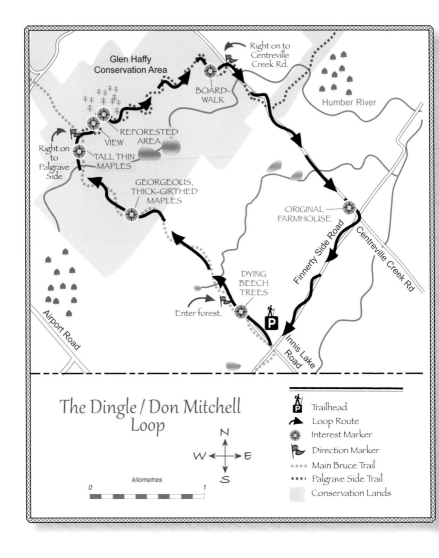

The Dingle / Don Mitchell Loop

N
W — E
S

kilometres

0   1

- Trailhead
- Loop Route
- Interest Marker
- Direction Marker
- Main Bruce Trail
- Palgrave Side Trail
- Conservation Lands

Map labels: Glen Haffy Conservation Area · Right on to Centreville Creek Rd. · BOARD-WALK · Humber River · REFORESTED AREA · VIEW · Right on to Palgrave Side · TALL THIN MAPLES · GEORGEOUS, THICK-GIRTHED MAPLES · ORIGINAL FARMHOUSE · Finnerty Side Road · Centreville Creek Rd · DYING BEECH TREES · Enter forest. · Airport Road · Innis Lake Road · P

*"Thousands of tired, nerve-shaken, over-civilized people
are beginning to find out that going to the mountains
is going home; that wildness is a necessity"*

JOHN MUIR

The Dingle/
Don Mitchell Loop

OVERVIEW

This loop is a favourite among members of a group with whom I used to hike every Sunday morning. It is flat, passes through lovely forest, and both Centreville Creek Road and Finnerty Side Road are quiet and feature a number of fine houses to look at. We found it nice to be able to walk side by side and chat since we called these hikes "Walk and Talk." Many a time, I'd find myself deep in conversation with Don Mitchell while strolling along this route. Don was one of the group's dedicated members and he lived nearby. We'd mostly discuss issues affecting Caledon since Don was a keen member of the Caledon Countryside Alliance, and I was its founder and executive director at the time. Don died in 2011, and when I walk this route I remember his sage and generous advice as well as his get-up-in-the-morning-and-put-your-best-foot-forward demeanor.

A dingle is a wooded or deep gulch that is shadowed from the sun. The Dingle School, SS#11, which is near here, was first a log and then a brick schoolhouse. Finnerty Side Road is named after Michael Finnerty, an early settler.

Directions

1. Park on Innis Lake Road just north of Finnerty Side Road.

2. Walk north on Innis Lake Road until it comes to a dead end. Follow the white blazes of the main Bruce Trail as it enters the woods and begins a gentle descent.

3. You walk through a lovely forest where sunshine filters through the canopy. There are a number of huge maples with girths worthy of a storybook grandma. Note there are old-growth maples with two very different shapes. Some have branches nearer the ground that extend out and make great shade. Later you see big maples where the lowest branches are way up in the air. The difference is due to their upbringing. The shady maples were single children growing up in open fields so they spread out. The taller ones were raised with lots of siblings all about them so they had to put their energy into growing tall to get the sunshine needed for photosynthesis.

4. About 3k into the hike, you come to a stile where the Palgrave Side Trail and its blue blazes leaves the main Bruce Trail. Climb over the stile and follow the Palgrave Side Trail.

5. You leave the forest coming out into an area where there is a nice sweeping view and a great bench to sit on and take in your surroundings. I wished I'd had a thermos of coffee with me at this peaceful spot as it was very early in the morning when I passed by.

6. You go through several reforested areas. One, in particular, has been thinned out. While most reforested areas have no undergrowth, this one is alive with bushes and hardwoods that have responded to the sun that now penetrates the canopy.

7. Cross a small service road before walking along some boardwalks and arriving at Centreville Creek Road.

8. Turn right on to Centreville Creek Road, following this quiet, hilly gravel road.

9. After 2k, you arrive at Finnerty Side Road. On your right just before the intersection, there is a small grey farmhouse that was recently restored. Its 1½-storey architecture is typical of this area that was originally settled by immigrants from Ireland.

10. Turn right on to Finnerty Side Road for a little over 1.5k until it arrives at Innis Lake Road and your vehicle.

Rushes.

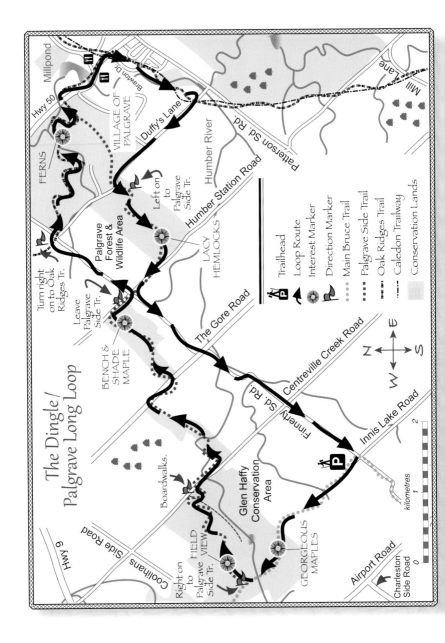

The Dingle / Palgrave Long Loop

VILLAGE OF PALGRAVE

Hwy 50

Millpond

FERNS

Brawton Dr.

Duffy's Lane

Humber River

Patterson Sd. Rd.

Mill Lane

Left on to Palgrave Side Tr.

LACY HEMLOCKS

Humber Station Road

Palgrave Forest & Wildlife Area

Turn right on to Oak Ridges Tr.

Leave Palgrave Side Tr.

BENCH & SHADE MAPLE

The Gore Road

Centreville Creek Road

Finnerty Sd. Rd.

Innis Lake Road

Boardwalks

Glen Haffy Conservation Area

Right on to Palgrave Side Tr.

FIELD VIEW

GEORGEOUS MAPLES

Hwy 9

Coolihans Side Road

Airport Road

Charleston Side Road

Legend

- Trailhead
- Loop Route
- Interest Marker
- Direction Marker
- Main Bruce Trail
- Palgrave Side Trail
- Oak Ridges Trail
- Caledon Trailway
- Conservation Lands

N E W S

kilometres
0   1   2

The Dingle / Palgrave Long Loop

OVERVIEW

I hadn't planned to walk so far when I hiked this route, but the path was there in front of me so I just kept going. It's amazing that a place so close to Toronto has such a long footpath through the countryside. It goes on and on in the best of ways until you come to Palgrave where you can have a latte (except on Sundays) or visit The Church pub. Now that's my kind of a hike – and my kind of church.

As I left Palgrave, I met a man carrying a big backpack. I told him he looked like a pilgrim en route to Compostela in Spain. Turns out he was training for his third trip along the famous Camino. We exchanged stories since I walked the route in 2004.

This trail passes through The Dingle, which is a wooded or deep gulch that is shadowed from the sun. First constructed from logs and then bricks, the Dingle School, SS#11, served this area, which was mostly settled by the Irish.

Be warned, this route took me almost seven hours. It's not hilly, but it's long.

*"All walking is discovery.
On foot we take the time to see things whole."*

HAL BORLAND

Nicola's
Insider Info

LENGTH
25 kilometres

LEVEL OF DIFFICULTY
Moderate

LENGTH OF TIME
6 to 9 hours

NUMBER OF STEPS
33,872

kCAL BURNED 1,095

HIGHLIGHTS
Length of trail, fishway, millpond, Palgrave, large maples and black cherries

PLACES TO EAT/DRINK
Palgrave Café
(closed Sundays),
Palgrave Variety Store,
The Church pub (Wed to Sun, 4pm to 12pm)

ENTRANCE FEE
n/a

GPS

TRAIL MARKER
Loop 36

In Appreciation of
Rotary Club of Palgrave

Directions

1. Park on Innis Lake Road just north of Finnerty Side Road.

2. Walk north on Innis Lake Road until it ends. Follow the white blazes of the main Bruce Trail as it enters the woods and begins a gentle descent.

3. You walk through a lovely forest with maples of all shapes and sizes.

4. About 3k later, you come to a stile where the Palgrave Side Trail and its blue blazes leaves the main Bruce Trail. Climb over the stile and follow the Palgrave Side Trail.

Bruce Trail marker.

5. When you leave the forest, look over the vista and stop for a break at a well-placed bench.

6. Cross a service road, pass over some boardwalks and arrive at Centreville Creek Road.

7. Cross Centreville Creek Road, turn right, following the blue blazes. After 500m, the trail goes left away from the road.

8. The trail passes through some wet areas where the Palgrave Rotary Club has paid for a system of boardwalks that protect the environment and keep your shoes dry. This active Rotary Club holds an annual wine tasting event in Palgrave that is well attended and lots of fun.

9. Cross The Gore Road, turn right and follow the road for about 500m. The trail once again dips back into the countryside to your left.

10. Just before you arrive at Humber Station Road, there is another bench to sit on. This time it's by an enormous maple that is the best shade maple I've ever seen. It's a beauty. Time for tea?

11. At Humber Station Road turn right and walk to the intersection with Finnerty Side Road. The Palgrave Side Trail continues straight on Humber Station Road, but you will turn left and follow Finnerty Side Road, leaving the blue blazes behind.

12. The next road you come to is Duffy's Lane. Cross it and immediately on your right (the southeast corner of the intersection) there is a sign for the Oak Ridges Trail with its white blazes.

13. Turn right into the forest, following the Oak Ridges Trail. It goes both straight ahead and to the left. Go straight ahead, paralleling Duffy's Lane. You follow numbered signs through this section. Here is a list of what to do at each sign:

▶	19	right		15	cross bridge
▲	18	straight	◀	14	left
◀	17	left	◀	13	left
▲	16	straight	◀	10	left

14. Follow the Oak Ridges Trail and its white blazes for about 3k through the Palgrave Forest and Wildlife Area turning as directed above. Keep an eye open for mountain bikers who use this trail.

15. After 3k you arrive at a junction between the Oak Ridges Trail that you are now following and the Palgrave Side Trail that you were on earlier. The Palgrave Side Trail ends here. Turn left continuing to follow the Oak Ridges Trail and its white blazes.

16. When you arrive at Highway 50, cross it with caution and turn right on the far side. At the end of the guardrail, the Oak Ridges Trail leaves Highway 50 and follows a wire fence.

17. After 400m, you come to the Palgrave Rotary Parking Lot where there is an information sign and gazebo. Continue on to the large millpond. This millpond is the result of a dam on the Humber River. Each winter, Palgrave's "Ice Angel" (aka Ken Hunt) maintains the ice rink. He began the practice when he couldn't find another venue where his children could skate. The rinks are open to anyone who wants to use them at their own risk. There are benches and washrooms, most of which were paid for by the Palgrave Rotary Club. There are hockey tournaments and other events held on the ice, which makes the winter a much more enjoyable season for many Caledon residents.

18. The trail goes under Highway 50 and crosses the dam that is responsible for the millpond.

19. The trail returns to Highway 50 and heads into the village.

20. Stop for "provisions" at the Palgrave Café, the new Church pub or the Palgrave Variety. The café serves lunch and – so kindly – lattes.

21. After a break, continue south on Highway 50 past the gas station until you come to a grapevine-covered trellis that marks the Caledon Trailway/Oak Ridges Trail.

22. Turn right and follow the Caledon Trailway/Oak Ridges Trail. This is where I met a man training to walk Spain's famous Camino. Cross Brawton Drive.

23. When you come to the trestle bridge that goes over Duffy's Lane, leave the Caledon Trailway/Oak Ridges Trail by taking a small trail that heads down to the road. It is on the left side of the path before the trestle bridge. The distance between the trellis and Duffy's Lane is 1.5k.

24. Turn right and walk north on Duffy's Lane. Practically underneath the overpass is a large sign for Deerfields Stables Country Inn. This "Private Club" is now a retreat centre that specializes in managing the biological aging process. Yikes! Its best feature, in my opinion however, is its Gypsy vanner horses. These black and white darlings are a sight with their long flowing manes and tails, and feathery legs.

25. After about 2k, you come to the Palgrave Side Trail again. This time, turn left and follow its blue blazes as it meanders through a lovely forest with some great old maples and enormous black cherry trees. You pass a pond and all too soon come to Humber Station Road.

26. Turn right on to Humber Station Road.

27. When you come to Finnerty Side Road (about 1k later), turn left and follow Finnerty Side Road. It crosses The Gore Road, Centreville Creek Road and finally takes you back to Innis Lake Road after about an hour. While this is more road walking than I like, it's a small price to pay for 18 or more kilometres of trail, and it's a great walking road. Finnerty Side Road is unpaved with a wide shoulder, few cars and an abundance of beautiful homes to admire.

28. When you get to Innis Lake Road, your car should be waiting. I predict you will be pooped out.

Valleywood Loop

You will be amazed by the variety of birdlife along this route.

Nicola's
Insider Info

LENGTH
2.8 kilometres

LEVEL OF DIFFICULTY
Easy

LENGTH OF TIME
45 minutes to 1 hour

NUMBER OF STEPS
4,680

kCAL BURNED 151

HIGHLIGHTS
Large healthy wetland complex, birds, walking under Highway 410

PLACES TO EAT/DRINK
Broadway Farm's Market or Downey's Farm Market on Heart Lake Road north of Mayfield Road

ENTRANCE FEE
n/a

OVERVIEW

Many people will be surprised to learn that Caledon has several Brampton-like subdivisions. In its southern reaches and, unfortunately, on top of some of the best agricultural land in Canada, sit a number of high-density subdivisions. This walk leaves from a small parkette in Valleywood, a community on the east side of Highway 10 / Hurontario Street, just north of Mayfield Road, where cul de sacs, courts and crescents abound. While Valleywood may not sound like a very promising place to hike, this short route travels through a spectacular wetland in the Etobicoke Creek watershed. Moreover, it has the richest birdlife of any of the routes I travelled for this guide. Flocks of goldfinches flitted along beside me; swallows swooped in search of insects and sparrows chirped my passing. I saw a great blue heron, ducks and a scarlet tanager. Stop and watch the birds in this little oasis.

GPS

TRAIL MARKER
Loop 37

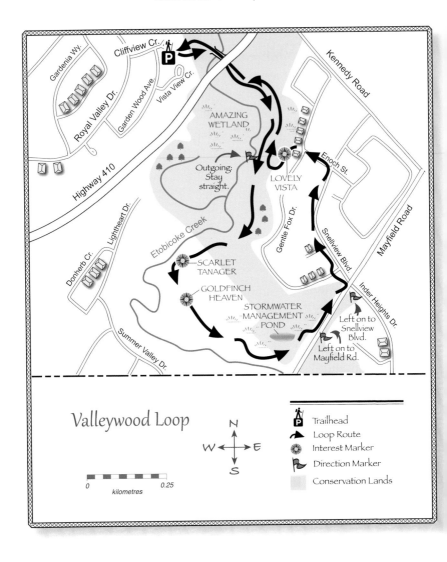

Valleywood Loop

N
W — E
S

0   0.25
kilometres

🚶 Trailhead
➤ Loop Route
✳ Interest Marker
🚩 Direction Marker
▨ Conservation Lands

"It is not talking but walking that will bring us to heaven."

MATTHEW HENRY

Etobicoke Creek valley.

Directions

1. Enter Valleywood via Royal Valley Drive. Turn right on to Cliffview Crescent and follow it until it ends at Newhouse Park. Park here.

2. A paved path leads down a slope that I suppose is the "cliff" in Cliffview Crescent. It travels to the right as you look over the valley. Follow it down.

3. Stay on this path as it veers right, becomes a cinder trail and crosses a bridge over Etobicoke Creek. Etobicoke is a Mississauga word that means "place where alders grow." Etobicoke Creek flows into Lake Ontario, dividing Toronto and Mississauga.

4.	After a short distance, you pass under Highway 410, which is a bit eerie.

5.	Continue following the cinder path through this wetland. There are several ponds, and birds abound. I had an all-too-rare sighting of a scarlet tanager (*Piranga olivacea*). A member of the cardinal family, these brilliantly red birds are a dullish olive colour when not breeding. I followed dozens of goldfinches as they flitted from burdock to goldenrod, and there were sparrows and swallows and ducks. This hike offered the best birdlife of all the loops described in this guide. Who would have thought!

6.	Soon, as this is not a long trail, you pass a large storm-water management pond on your left, then the trail empties on to Mayfield Road. Turn left on to Mayfield Road. Stay on the paved path, which keeps you on the left side of this busy street. Fortunately, you follow it for less than 200m, so you will survive.

7.	Turn left on to Snellview Blvd. Snelgrove is a nearby town that was named after J.C. Snell, a successful farmer. He bred and raised shorthorn cattle, Cotswold sheep, Birkshire swine and more. Between 1878 and 1884 his livestock won more prizes at the Chicago Fat Stock Show than any other Canadian exhibitor.

8.	Follow Snellview Blvd. past some brand-spanking new houses that sell for $650,000 or more until you come to Enoch Street.

9.	Turn left on to Enoch Street beside the playground.

10.	Cross Gentle Fox Drive and pass through the alleyway that is straight ahead. It goes between two houses.

11.	From behind these homes, you have a great view of the wetland below.

12.	Follow the cinder path down the hill until it meets the cinder path you took on your outward journey.

13.	Turn right at this T-intersection of trails.

14.	You pass under the 410 again and cross over the bridge.

15.	Soon you climb back up the "cliff" to Newhouse Park and your vehicle.

We Want Your Feedback

Hiking routes evolve over time. If you find a route has changed or uncover an error in the directions included in this guide, please send these corrections to me. Similarly, if you have suggestions for other loops, please let me know. If you simply want to share your hiking experiences along these routes, I'd love to hear from you. Finally, if you are interested in having me lead a hike for your group along one of these looproutes, please contact me at

nross@woodrising.com or visit **nicolaross.ca**

GPS
LOG

Hike Name/#	GPS Image Found	GPS Coordinates	Date	Notes

Keep a log of the GPS Trail Markers you find. When you have found 10 or more, send their GPS coordinates to **nross@woodrising.com** or visit **nicolaross.ca** to be entered to win a prize. Many smart phones have a GPS.

Acknowledgments

Writing a book is a long journey, but in the case of *Caledon Hikes* it hasn't been lonely. This guide is the combined effort of a team of friends and colleagues who have been generous, enthusiastic and diligent.

Over endless cups of coffee, my good friend John Denison talked me into focusing on loop routes. And to be sure my directions actually led hikers back to where they began, I relied on a baseball team of testers including Al Axworthy, Mary Ann Bowman, John Ford, Gail MacLennan, Nick Marshall, Peter Mckinney, Jen Palacios and Mike Vaselenak. Through rain and – literally – snow, they were out there making sure I didn't say left when I really meant right.

Barb Campbell, Angus & Sien Doughty, Richard Ehrlich and Neil Morris suggested routes in regions less familiar to me, and when it came to errant commas Al Axworthy, Mary Ann Bowman, Janet Kimantas, and Alex Strachan were eagle-like. Julian Mulock offered to paint the cover image, and Angela Larsen, Amy Darrell and Gary Hall pitched in with some stunning photographs.

Gill Stead, the book's designer, gracefully worked her magic while prodding me to stay on schedule and coaching me on the minutiae of map making.

Nancy Frater at Booklore and Don Coats at Caledon Hills Cycling put the first demo copies on their shelves, seemingly as proud as I was to have *Caledon Hikes* on display. Signe Ball at *In the Hills* magazine and Ned Morgan at *Mountain Life* generously promoted the book, while countless friends and colleagues talked it up in their newsletters, blogs, websites and while chatting with family and friends.

My pal Cheryl Mitchell never complained when I took over her kitchen table with my computer, GPS, camera and other hiking paraphernalia. In fact, she'd often stick a smoothie under my nose and say "drink!"

Formerly a Catholic Church,
now a residence.
PHOTO BY AMY DARRELL

Forks of the Credit maple. PHOTO BY ANGELA LARSON

Thanks also to the individual hike sponsors. I hope our collaboration helps you too. (*See page 189 for a list of sponsors.*)

And, of course, this book relies on the tireless efforts, much of it by volunteers, of the Bruce Trail Conservancy, the Humber Valley Heritage Trail Association, the Caledon Trailway, the Elora Cataract Trailway, the Oak Ridges Trail Association, the Grand Valley Trail Association, Credit Valley Conservation, Toronto and Region Conservation Authority, and Ontario Parks, all of which have footpaths within Caledon's borders.

Finally, my partner and patron Alex Strachan kicked my writing butt into gear, encouraging me to get out there and write another book.

My sincerest thanks to everyone involved. A bit of each of you is embedded in every last page of **Caledon Hikes**.

About the Author

R aised in Caledon on southern Ontario's Niagara Escarpment in Toronto's urban shadow, Nicola Ross developed a keen sense of place at an early age. She attended the Belfountain Public School and Mayfield Secondary School, topping off her formal education with a BSc in biology from the University of Guelph. Then it was off to see the world and to pursue her career in environmental studies.

After living away for more than a decade and a half, Nicola returned to Belfountain, the Niagara Escarpment and her beloved Credit River. She created the Caledon Countryside Alliance (CCA) to engage citizens in stewarding the area's precious countryside. Among its programs, the CCA hosted hikes along Caledon's plethora of trails and country roads. These weekly outings encouraged participants to see Caledon from the inside out.

Nicola also discovered the benefits and joys of adding a pen to her environmental battles. Before long she was writing feature articles on environmental topics for *In the Hills* magazine. Another decade-and-a-half later, she is one of the magazine's most regular contributors, as well as the award-winning author of five books, including *Caledon*, *Dufferin County*, *Healing the Landscape* and *The Carrying Place Trail*. She has published articles in *The Walrus*, *The Globe and Mail*, *explore* magazine, *Mountain Life* and more. Formerly, the editor-in-chief of *Alternatives Journal*, Canada's national environmental magazine, Nicola is now pursuing her love of writing, travel, sport and Caledon on a full time basis.

nicolaross.ca • nross@woodrising.com • blog.nicolaross.ca

Generous Sponsors

Caledon Hikes: Loops & Lattes is more of a community project than a book. Myriad businesses, organizations and hikers have been part of its creation. A few of them went a step further and actually sponsored a hike or two.

THE LODGE AT PINE COVE
Discover the French River

Possibility grows here

IN THE HILLS

My thanks to The Lodge at Pine Cove,
Caledon Hills Cycling, Friends of the Greenbelt Foundation,
In the Hills magazine, Spirit Tree Estate Cidery, The Farmhouse Pottery
and others who have made this guide possible and so much fun.

I encourage you to frequent their businesses when possible.

Nicola Ross